Multisensory
Theme-A-Saurus

The great big book of sensory learning

D1288992

by **Gayle Bittinger**

Illustrated by **Gary Mohrman**

Totline® Publications
A Division of Frank Schaffer Publications, Inc.
Torrance, California

We wish to thank the following teachers, childcare workers, and parents for contributing some of the ideas in this book: Jacqueline Abbott, East Greenbush, NY; Ellen Bedford, Bridgeport, CT; John M. Bittinger, Everett, WA; Janice Bodenstedt, Jackson, MI; Kim Bohl, Adrian, MI; Patty Claycomb, Ventura, CA; Barbara Conahan, Hazleton, PA; Marjorie Debowy, Stony Brook, NY; Jeanette Flagge, Fort Dodge, IA; Barbara Fletcher, El Cajon, CA; Lisa Fransen, Eden Prairie, MN; Rosemary Giordano, Philadelphia, PA; Cathy B. Griffin, Plainsboro, NJ; Lanette L. Gutierrez, Olympia, WA; Gemma Hall-Hart, Bellingham, WA; Peggy Hanley, St. Joseph, MI; Mary Haynes, Lansing, MI; Mildred Hoffman, Tacoma, WA; Colraine Pettipaw Hunley, Doyleston, PA; Margo Hunter, Westerville, OH; Barbara H. Jackson, Denton, TX; Kathy McCullough, St. Charles, IL; Judith McNitt, Adrian, MI; Kathy Monahan, Coon Rapids, MN; Susan M. Paprocki, Northbrook, IL; Susan Peters, Upland, CA; Dawn Picolelli, Wilmington, DE; Lois E. Putnam, Pilot Mountain, NC; Beverly Qualheim, Marquette, MI; Sue Schliecker, Waukesha, WI; Betty Silkunas, Lansdale, PA; Jacki Smallwood, Royersford, PA; Jane M. Spannbauer, South St. Paul, MN; Diane Thom, Maple Valley, WA; Cathi Ulbright, Wooster, OH; Barbara Vilet, Cortland, IL; Kristine Wagoner, Puyallup, WA; Peggy Wolf, Pittsburgh, PA; JoAnn Yamada, Port Hueneme, CA; Maryann Zucker, Reno, NV; Deborah Zumbar, Alliance, OH.

Managing Editor: Kathleen Cubley

Contributing Editors: Susan Hodges, Elizabeth McKinnon, Jean Warren

Copyeditor: Mae Rhodes

Proofreader: Kris Fulsaas

Book Design/Layout: Sarah Ness, Gordon Frazier

Cover Design: Brenda Mann Harrison

Cover Illustration: Kathy Kotomaimoce

Production Manager: JoAnna Haffner and Melody Olney

ISBN 1-57029-131-4
Library of Congress Catalog Number 96-60384
Printed in the United States of America

Published by Totline Publications
Editorial Office: P.O. Box 2250
                    Everett, WA 98203
Business Office: 23740 Hawthorne Blvd.
                    Torrance, CA 90505

20 19 18 17 16 15 14 13 12 11 10 9 8 7 6 5 4

Introduction

Young children learn best when all their senses are activated and involved. That's why the activities in *Multisensory Theme-A-Saurus* are perfect for them. Each learning concept or theme is presented with activities that involve seeing, touching, hearing, smelling, and tasting.

Your children will enjoy using their senses to learn and explore everything from colors and shapes to foods and nature. As you do the various activities with the children, talk about the concept or theme being emphasized. How are they seeing it with their eyes, touching it with their hands, listening to it with their ears, smelling it with their nose, and tasting it with their tongue?

As with all Totline Publications, the activities in this book use inexpensive, readily available materials, and they are appropriate for children 3 to 5 years old. Take the time to stop and smell, look, touch, taste, and hear the world with your children and the activities in *Multisensory Theme-A-Saurus.*

Contents

Foods

Environments

Nature

Animals

Red

Our Wagon Is Red

Set a red wagon in the middle of your room. Ask your children to look all around the room to find red objects to put in the wagon. When the wagon is full, encourage your children to notice all the different shades of red. Then let your children take turns pulling the wagon around the room to put the objects away.

Touching

Texture Shapes

For each of your children, cut a large shape out of heavy paper. Prepare a variety of red, textured objects for the children to glue on the shapes. For example, you could dye pasta or rice red (see recipe below), collect red fabric and ribbon scraps, and find shiny red wrapping paper or clear red cellophane. Set out the shapes and textured objects. Let the children spread glue all over their shapes and cover them with the various textured objects. When the glue has dried, have your children gently rub their hands across the shapes to feel the different textures.

Dyeing Pasta and Rice—Place a small amount of rubbing alcohol in a jar with a lid. Add a few drops of red food coloring. Fill the jar about two-thirds full with uncooked pasta or rice. Put on the lid and shake until the color is evenly distributed. Allow the pasta or rice to dry on paper towels for about an hour. (You may substitute water for rubbing alcohol. The color will be less intense, and the pasta or rice will need to dry overnight.)

I'm a Big Red Tomato

Sing this song about red tomatoes with your children. Encourage them to listen carefully for the word *red*. You may wish to sing this song before eating the soup from the Yum, Yum, Soup activity on this page.

Sung to: "Little White Duck"

I'm a big red tomato
Growing on the vine,
A big red tomato
Looking, oh, so fine.
Now you can make
Good things with me—
Soup, juice, pizza,
To name just three.
I'm a big red tomato
Growing on the vine.
Grow, grow, grow.

Jean Warren

Red Candy Scents

Make this smelling game for your children. Collect several different kinds of red candy, each with a different smell, such as cherry, strawberry, and watermelon drops and cinnamon red hots. For each kind of candy, place a small amount in two opaque containers with lids that let the scents out (empty yogurt containers with small holes in the lid work well). Mix up the containers. Using only their sense of smell, have your children take turns finding the matching containers of candy.

Yum, Yum, Soup

Purchase a can of Campbell's brand tomato soup. Show the can to your children. Ask them to point to the red on the label. Let the children help you make the soup. (Substitute one canful of milk for the water to make it extra creamy.) Serve each child a small serving of warm soup. Talk about the color of the soup. Then have the children taste their soup. Yum!

Yellow

School Bus Mural

Your children will love to see themselves "ride" the yellow
school bus in this mural. Cut a long school bus shape out
of white butcher paper. Cut a window out of the bus for
each child. Let your children work together to paint the bus
yellow. When the paint has dried, use a black felt tip marker
to add details. Attach the bus shape to a wall or a bulletin
board. Place photographs of the children in the windows,
one child per window. Have the children find themselves
on your "bus."

Touching

Measuring With Cornmeal

Pour yellow cornmeal into a plastic
dishpan. Set out spoons, measuring
cups, a funnel, and other utensils.
Encourage your children to practice
pouring and measuring the yellow
cornmeal. How many spoonfuls does
it take to fill up the smallest measuring
cup? The largest?

Star Search

Cut stars out of yellow construction paper and hide them around the room. Play or sing the song "Twinkle, Twinkle, Little Star" and have your children begin searching for the hidden stars. Let them continue searching as long as they hear the music. Have them stand still each time the music stops. Continue the game until all the stars have been found.

Variation: Let your children sing this version of "Twinkle, Twinkle, Little Star" while they are searching.

Twinkle, twinkle, yellow star,

How I wonder where you are.

Let's go looking here and there,

Let's go looking everywhere.

Twinkle, twinkle, yellow star,

How I wonder where you are.

Jean Warren

Smelling

Smells Like a Lemon

Make a batch of modeling dough using your favorite recipe (or the recipe that follows). Add a few drops of lemon flavoring to the completed dough. Let your children create with the scented dough. Talk about the lemon scent. Ask the children if they can think of other times they may have smelled that same scent: Lemonade? Lemon drops? Lemon pie?

Modeling Dough—Mix together 1 cup flour, 6 to 7 Tbsp. water, 1 Tbsp. vegetable oil, and several drops of food coloring. Knead until smooth. Store in an airtight container.

Tasting

Tasting Party

Have a yellow Tasting Party with your children. Set out as many different yellow foods as possible, such as banana pudding, lemonade, pineapple slices, corn muffins, and cooked corn. Let each child take a small amount of each to taste. Which food did they like best?

Blue

Blue Bubble Prints

In a small plastic container, mix one part blue liquid tempera paint with two parts liquid dishwashing detergent and stir in a small amount of water. Show your children how to blow through a straw. Have them practice this. Then, let one child at a time put his or her straw in the paint mixture and blow through it until the bubbles rise above the rim of the plastic container. What color are the bubbles? Lay a piece of white paper on top of the bubbles and let the child rub gently across it. As the bubbles pop, they will leave delicate blue prints on the paper.

Digging Fun

Fill a plastic dishpan partway with blue aquarium gravel. (Aquarium gravel can be purchased inexpensively at many pet stores.) Collect several small blue objects, such as a blue toy car, a blue crayon, and a blue rubber ball. Hide the blue objects in the gravel. Let your children take turns digging through the blue gravel with their hands to find the blue objects.

Little Boy Blue

Recite the nursery rhyme "Little Boy Blue" with your children. Encourage them to act out the motions as indicated.

Little Boy Blue,

Come blow your horn.
(Pretend to blow horn.)

The sheep's in the meadow.
(Point one way.)

The cow's in the corn.
(Point the other way.)

But where is the boy
(Cup hand over eye and look around.)

Who looks after the sheep?

He's under a haystack

Fast asleep.
(Pretend to sleep.)

Traditional

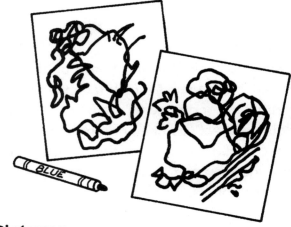

Smelling

Smelly Pictures

Collect as many blue, scented felt tip markers as possible. Depending on the number of markers you have, invite a few of your children over to a table. Take the lids off the markers and help the children carefully sniff the scents. Give each child a white or light blue sheet of construction paper. Let them use the "smelly" markers to make blue Smelly Pictures.

Tasting

Blueberry Muffins

Purchase a box of corn muffin mix. Let your children help you prepare the muffin batter according to the package directions. Add a handful of fresh or frozen blueberries and stir the batter gently. Pour the batter into muffin cups and bake as directed. Serve the muffins warm with butter. Encourage your children to notice the blue "dots" in their muffins while they eat them.

Orange

Orange Prints

Cut sponges into circles. To make paint pads, fold paper towels in half, place them in shallow containers, and pour on small amounts of orange tempera paint. Give each of your children a sheet of white or orange construction paper. Show your children how to press the sponge circles on the paint pads and then on the construction paper to make round "orange" prints. How many prints can they make?

Hearing

Something Orange

Sing the song below with your children. Have them follow the directions as indicated in the song. Then make up your own verses using the names of orange objects in your room and some appropriate directions.

Sung to: "If You're Happy and You Know It"

If you see an orange pumpkin, touch it now.

If you see an orange pumpkin, touch it now.

If you see an orange pumpkin,

If you see an orange pumpkin,

If you see an orange pumpkin, touch it now.

Marjorie Debowy

Touching

Exploring Pumpkins

Set out several different sizes of pumpkins for your children to explore. Point out the orange color as the children feel the outsides of the pumpkins. Which pumpkin is the heaviest? Which is the lightest? Cut open one of the pumpkins. Let the children help you take out the orange pulp. What does it feel like?

Pumpkin Pies

Cut pie shapes out of orange construction paper. Set out a container of pumpkin pie spice. Have your children brush glue all over their pie shapes. Then let them sprinkle pumpkin pie spice all over their shapes to make fragrant "pumpkin pies."

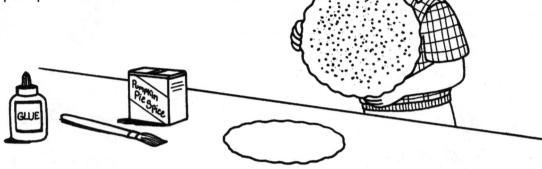

Tasting

Orange Lemonade

Add red food coloring to water in a clear glass or plastic pitcher. Pour the water into ice cube trays and freeze. When the ice cubes are partially frozen, make lemonade with your children. Give each child a glass of lemonade, a red ice cube to put in it, and a small spoon. As the children stir their lemonade, discuss what happens to the color and why. When the ice is all melted, let the children taste their orange-colored lemonade.

Green

Green Hair Cups

Set out plain (green, if possible) paper cups, felt tip markers, a bucket of dirt with a small shovel or a spoon, some
grass seed, and a spray bottle filled with water. Have each
of your children use the felt tip markers to draw a face on a
paper cup. As the children finish, have them fill their paper
cups with dirt. Help them sprinkle on some grass seed and
water the seed with the spray bottle. Place the cups in a
sunny window. Have the children check their cups regularly
to see if they need watering and to watch for green grass
sprouting. When the grass has grown several inches high,
show the children how to use scissors to trim it like "hair."

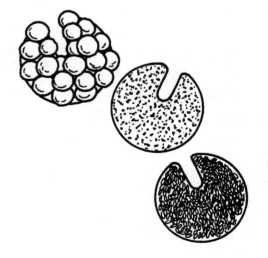

Touching

Little Green Frogs

Cut lily pad shapes out of green construction paper. Glue
different-textured items, such as cotton balls, sand, and
rice, onto the lily pads. Tape the lily pads to the floor all
around your room. Have your children pretend to be frogs.
Ask them to "ribbit" as they hop from lily pad to lily pad.
Which lily pad do they like to touch the most?

Variation: Cut some of the lily pads out of other colors. Tape
them to floor as well. Ask your "frogs" to only jump onto
the green lily pads.

Did You Ever See a Lizard?

Sing the following song with your children. Have them clap each time they hear the word *green*.

Sung to: "Did You Ever See a Lassie?"

Did you ever see a lizard,

A lizard, a lizard—

Did you ever see a lizard

All dressed up in green?

With green eyes and green nose

And green legs and green toes—

Did you ever see a lizard

All dressed up in green?

Kim Heckert

Green Herbs

Collect a variety of herbs for your children to smell. If possible, have both fresh and dried herbs available. Talk about the different scents. Which one do they like best? Make a bar graph showing the children's preferences.

Extension: Use several of the Italian herbs, such as oregano and basil, to turn plain tomato sauce into pasta sauce. Serve over cooked plain or spinach pasta.

Herbs We Like	
Mint	✔✔✔✔✔
Basil	✔✔
Oregano	
Parsley	✔✔✔
Thyme	✔✔
Dill	✔✔✔

Green Snack

Prepare a bag of frozen green peas according to package directions. Allow the peas to cool slightly. Give each of your children a paper plate. Let the children take turns scooping a small amount of the peas onto their plates. Talk about the green color, and let the children enjoy the taste of the green peas.

Purple

Red and Blue Make Purple

Give each of your children a sheet of fingerpaint paper. On each sheet of paper, put a dollop of red fingerpaint and a dollop of blue fingerpaint. Encourage your children to use their fingers and hands to mix the red and blue paint together. Have them watch as the blue and red paint turn into purple.

Touching

Purple Shape Parade

Cut large shapes out of purple construction paper and tape them to the floor. Tie purple crepe-paper streamers to your children's wrists. Play some music and have the children walk, march, hop, or dance across the shapes on the floor.

Variation: Let your children bounce balls on the shapes or use them as "stepping stones" in a start-to-finish game.

Purple Story

Give each of your children a half sheet of purple construction paper. Explain to the children that you will be telling them a "purple" story. Every time they hear the word *purple*, they are to wave their purple papers in the air. Begin your made-up purple story. Each time you say the word *purple*, pause and let the children wave their papers.

Tasting

Grapes and Raisins

Give each of your children a small bunch of purple grapes and a handful of raisins. Let the children taste each of them. What do the grapes taste like? How do the raisins taste? Do the raisins and grapes taste the same? Explain to the children that raisins are grapes that have been dried. Let the children finish their grape and raisin snack.

Smelling

Purple Flowers

Collect an assortment of purple flowers, such as irises, lilacs, and violets. Let your children sniff the various flowers. Do they all smell the same? Which one do they like the best? Let the children help you arrange the flowers in vases around the room, so they can sniff them throughout the day.

Brown

Seeing

Nut Collection

Show your children an assortment of brown nuts. Point out the different shades of brown that can be seen on the various kinds of nuts. Give each child a handful of the nuts. Ask the children to sort their nuts by kind. Then have them arrange the nuts in order from largest to smallest or from lightest brown to darkest brown.

Extension: Have your children help you shell the nuts. Let them use the shells to make a brown collage. Chop the nuts and serve them sprinkled over yogurt for a snack.

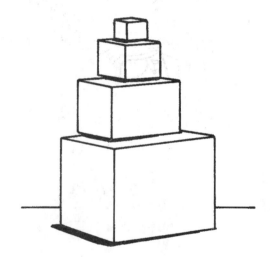

Touching

Stacking Boxes

Collect brown cardboard boxes in a variety of sizes. Tape the bottom and top of each box closed. Let your children use the boxes to build towers, houses, or any other structure they can think of. While they are building, ask them some questions about the boxes. Are some boxes heavier than others? Is it easier to carry a large box or a small box? What happens when you stack a large box on top of a small box?

Hearing

Rhythm Stick Fun

Collect two brown cardboard tubes for each of your children to use as rhythm sticks. Give each child a pair of the rhythm sticks. Explain to them that you will be saying the names of many colors. Whenever they hear *brown*, they should tap their brown rhythm sticks together. Whenever they hear any other color, they should hold their rhythm sticks still.

Cinnamon Dough Shapes

These shapes will keep their spicy scent for a long time.

$^3/_4$ cup ground cinnamon

1 cup applesauce

1 Tbsp. ground nutmeg

1 Tbsp. ground allspice

1 Tbsp. ground cloves

Mix all of the ingredients together until they form a smooth dough. Give each of your children a small piece of the dough. Let them roll and shape the dough as they wish. Encourage them to talk about the scent of the dough. Does the smell remind them of anything? When they are finished playing with the dough, help them roll it out to a $^1/_4$-inch thickness and cut out a shape with a cookie cutter. Place the shapes on waxed paper and poke a hole in the top of each shape. Allow the shapes to air-dry for several days. Turn the shapes often to prevent curling. Tie on loops of ribbon or yarn for hangers to complete.

Cinnamon Toast

Toast a slice of bread for each of your children. Ask the children to compare their toasted bread with plain bread. Which one is more brown? Help the children spread butter or margarine on their toast. Let the children take turns sprinkling a small amount of cinnamon sugar on their toast. Then let them enjoy the taste of the brown Cinnamon Toast.

Black

Carbon Copies

Put a sheet of black carbon paper between two sheets of plain white paper. Staple the pages together on the left hand side and write a small x on the side that should be written on (the side that will allow the carbon paper to make a copy on the bottom sheet of paper). Prepare several of these ahead of time. Invite several of your children to join you. Give each child one of the carbon sets. Let the children use pencils to draw on the top papers. Encourage them to press firmly. Then have them lift up the top page and the carbon paper to see the identical picture on the bottom page.

Black Handprints

Set out black washable tempera paint and several paintbrushes. Help your children paint the palms of their hands black. How does the paint feel? Does it tickle when it's brushed on? When their hands are completely covered with black paint, have the children press them on sheets of heavy paper to make handprints. Label each set of handprints with the child's name and the date. When the paint dries, let the children take their handprints home as gifts.

Variation: Instead of making handprints on individual sheets of paper, make a handprint mural for your room on a sheet of butcher paper.

Black Bat, Black Bat

Have your children pretend they are black bats, while you recite the following rhyme. Have them listen carefully and act out the movements as you name them. If you wish, give each child a black bat shape to hold as they move around.

Black bat, black bat, turn around.

Black bat, black bat, touch the ground.

Black bat, black bat, reach up high.

Black bat, black bat, touch the sky.

Black bat, black bat, reach down low.

Black bat, black bat, fly just so.

Adapted Traditional

Smelling

Licorice Scents

Make three smelling cups with red licorice bits and four smelling cups with black licorice bits. (See page 45 for directions on making smelling cups, if needed.) Place one of the black licorice cups on a sheet of black construction paper. Invite one of your children to smell the cup on the paper. Ask the child to smell the remaining cups and put the ones with the matching scent on the black paper.

Tasting

Licorice Straws

Cut the ends off black licorice vines to make straws. Have your children use the straws to drink their beverage at snacktime. When their drinks are all gone, let them eat their tasty straws.

White

Seeing

White Clouds

Take your children outside when there are white, fluffy clouds. Let them lie down on the ground and look up at the clouds. Help them see the different shapes the clouds make. Are the clouds changing and moving? Take them inside and let them make cloud pictures. Give each child a sheet of blue construction paper and a sheet of white construction paper. Show the children how to tear their white paper into cloud shapes to glue on their blue paper.

Touching

White Goo

In a dishpan, mix two parts cornstarch with one part water. Let your children take turns putting their hands in the "goo." What happens when they squish a handful of it? What does it feel like when they let it run through their fingers? Help your children come up with words to describe the goo.

Hearing

What Is It?

Collect as many white-colored balls as you can, such as a golf ball, a Ping-Pong ball, a softball, and a volleyball. Show your children the balls. Bounce each one up and down and have them listen carefully to the sound each one makes. Now stretch a blanket or a sheet between two chairs to make a screen. Bounce one of the balls behind the blanket and ask the children to tell you which ball it was. Repeat for each ball.

Scented Soap

Give each of your children a bowl with about ½ cup of laundry soap powder (not laundry detergent) and 1 to 2 tablespoons of water. Let the children mix their soap and water together. Talk about the smell of the soap as the children work with it. Give each child a 24-inch length of yarn. Have them fold their yarn pieces in half. Show them how to mold the soap and water mixture into a ball shape around the ends of the yarn to make soap-on-a-rope. Allow the soaps to dry overnight before hanging them up.

Tasting

Cottage Cheese Dip

Whirl cottage cheese in a blender and add sour cream or milk to make a thick, creamy mixture. For flavor, add ranch salad dressing to taste. Refrigerate for 30 minutes. Serve with raw vegetables.

Many Colors

My Color Book

Staple white sheets of construction paper together to make a book for each of your children. Write "(Child's name)'s Color Book" on the cover. At the top of each page, write a different color name, using a felt tip marker of that color. Choose a different color each day and let the children decorate the page with things of that color. For example, if you chose the color green, you could have your children make designs with green crayons or felt tip markers, attach green stickers, or glue on green pictures from magazines.

Touching

Finger-Color Matching

Attach circle stickers of several colors to your children's right fingertips, and matching stickers to their left fingertips. Have them match up their two red fingertips, then their two yellow fingertips, etc. Divide the children into pairs and have them try matching colored fingertips with their partners.

Variation: Set out objects that match the colors of the circle stickers on the children's fingertips. Let the children take turns touching a red object with a red finger, a yellow object with a yellow finger, and so on.

Hearing

Color Song

Have your children listen carefully to the following song. If they are wearing the color of the item named, have them follow the directions as they are sung. Repeat the song using other colors and articles of clothing.

Sung to: "Frère Jacques"

Children with red shoes,

Children with red shoes,

Please stand up, please stand up.

Clap your hands and turn around.

Clap your hands and turn around.

Then sit down, then sit down.

Betty Silkunas

Scratch and Sniff Paints

Add drops of flavoring extracts to tempera paints and set them out at an easel. Match the flavors with the paint colors: strawberry or cherry for red, banana or lemon for yellow, peppermint for green, orange for orange, chocolate for brown, anise for black, etc. Let your children use these paints at the easel for a colorful sensory experience.

Tasting

Fruit Salad Recipe

Prepare a variety of red, green, yellow, and orange fruits for a fruit salad. Put each fruit into a separate bowl. Make a recipe chart, as shown. Explain that the three red spoons mean to add three spoonfuls of red fruit, the green spoon means to add one spoonful of green fruit, and so on. Have the children make their fruit salads according to the recipe. When their salads are complete, let them enjoy tasting their colorful creations.

Fruit Salad

Red
Green
Yellow
Orange

Circles

Seeing

Circle Hunt

Place a Hula Hoop in the middle of the room. Point out the circle shape of the hoop to your children. Ask them to find other objects in the room that are the same shape. Have them put those objects inside the hoop. Let the children look at all the round objects they have found.

Touching

Coin Fun

Set out a collection of coins. Let your children play with the coins. What shape are they? Which coins have smooth edges? Which ones have rough edges? Encourage your children to stack and count the coins. If you wish, have the children make paper and crayon rubbings of the different coins. Encourage them to point out the circles on their rubbings.

Hearing

Ring Around the Rosie

Have your children arrange themselves in a circle and hold hands. Point out the shape they have just made. Now play Ring Around the Rosie, but instead of saying *ring* around the rosie, say a movement word such as *skip* or *tiptoe*. Have the children listen carefully, then move around in a circle in that way.

Hint: You may wish to mark a large circle on your floor with masking tape to make it easier for your children to stay in a circle.

Circle Pizzas

Prepare ingredients for making English muffin pizzas, including English muffin halves, tomato or pizza sauce, grated cheese, sliced pepperoni, sliced olives, cooked sausage, and any other toppings you wish to have. Help your children make their pizzas by spooning a little sauce onto their round muffins and adding the desired toppings. Encourage the children to smell each topping before putting it on their muffins. Are any of the toppings round as well? Place the muffins on baking sheets and broil until the cheese melts. Can the children smell the pizzas baking? Is there any topping they can smell more than another? Allow the pizzas to cool slightly before eating.

Circle Snacks

Select a variety of round foods to serve on a plastic turntable. You could include such foods as round crackers, oranges sliced into rounds, cucumber chips, circles cut out of cheese slices, and round egg slices. Let your children gently spin the turntable to select their round snack choices.

Squares

Checkerboard Fun

Set out a checkerboard and small squares cut from red and black construction paper. Point out the square shapes to your children. Let them take turns placing the red and black paper squares on the matching squares on the checkerboard.

Squared Away

On a smooth, washable surface, mark off several 9-inch squares with masking tape. Place a small amount of fingerpaint inside each square. Invite several of your children to sit in front of the squares (one child per square). Encourage the children to use their fingers to trace around the edges of their squares. Can they use their fingers to draw squares in the fingerpaint? As the children finish, show them how to use construction paper squares to make prints of their fingerpainted designs.

Square Song

Sing the following song with your children. Have them draw squares in the air as you sing the last line of the song.

Sung to: "London Bridge"

Squares have four equal sides,

Equal sides, equal sides.

Squares have four equal sides,

One, two, three, four.

Barbara Conahan

My Nose Knows

Collect three objects that smell, such as a flower, an orange, and some grass clippings. On the left-hand side of a large piece of paper, draw a picture of each item. Draw small boxes next to each picture to make a modified bar graph. Using construction paper, cut squares the size of the squares on your graph. Write each child's name on one of the squares. Pass out the squares. Talk about the smelly items shown on the graph. Let your children take turns smelling the objects. Which one do they like the best? Then, one at a time, have your children come up and paste their paper square onto the square that follows the item they most like to smell.

Salty Squares

Arrange square saltine crackers or other square snack crackers on a square tray. Give each of your children a square napkin. Let the children select several square crackers to eat.

Triangles

Build a Triangle

Cut at least 16 small, identical equilateral triangles out of felt. (Equilateral means all sides are the same length.) Place a few of the triangles on a flannelboard. Have your children look at the triangles and notice that they all have three sides and three points. Now put four triangles together, as shown in the illustration, to make a larger triangle. How can they tell it is still a triangle? (It still has three sides and three points.) Set out the triangles and flannelboard for the children to explore. Encourage them to find ways to make bigger triangles using the smaller ones.

Touching

Cutting Triangles

Set out some scissors and triangles cut from several different kinds of paper. Show your children how to cut off the corners of the triangles to make smaller triangles. Let them cut as many triangles as they wish.

Extension: When they are finished, put all the cut triangles in a box and let your children use them to create a large triangle collage.

Musical Triangles

Find a musical triangle to play during this activity. Cut tri-angles, at least one for each child, out of construction paper and place them around the room—on the floor, on a table, on a wall, on a chair. Tell your children that when you play the triangle, you want them to march around the room. When they hear the triangle stop, have them stop marching and find just one triangle. Have the children replace their triangles where they found them. Begin playing the musical triangle again. Repeat as long as interest lasts.

Smelling

Toast Triangles

Toast slices of bread. Spread half the toast slices with straw-berry jelly and the other half with grape jelly. Cut the toast into triangles. Give each of your children one of each kind of toast triangle. Can they tell what flavors of jelly are on their triangles just by smelling? Let them taste their tri-angles to confirm their guesses.

Tasting

Triangle Snack

Let your children enjoy this shapely snack. Show your children how to fold square napkins in half diagonally to form triangles. Place an assortment of triangular foods on a tray. For example, you could serve triangular crackers, cheese slices cut into triangles, and triangular wedges of watermelon. Let each child select several foods to place on his or her napkin and enjoy.

Rectangles

Seeing

Printing Fun

Cut sponges into rectangles of different sizes. Pour tempera paint into shallow containers. Cover a table with a large sheet of butcher paper. Let your children press the rectangular sponges in the paint, then onto the paper to make prints. Have them notice the shape of the prints. Talk about how a rectangle has two short sides and two long sides. Can they point to the short sides of a rectangle? How about the long sides? When the children are finished making prints, hang up their rectangular art.

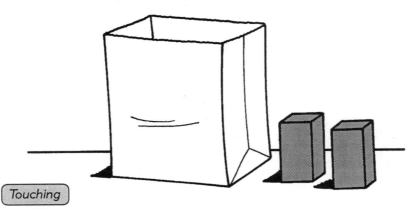

Touching

Match the Rectangles

Find rectangular blocks in several sizes, two of each size. Put the blocks into a paper bag. Let your children, one at a time, reach into the bag with both hands and find two matching blocks, just by using their sense of touch. Make sure each child has a turn to match the blocks.

Hearing

Find a Rectangle

As you sing this song, substitute the name of one of your children for *Molly*. When a child hears his or her name, have that child point to something in the room that is shaped like a rectangle.

Sung to: "Row, Row, Row Your Boat"

Point to a rectangle.

You'll find them all around—

A door, a book, just take a look.

Now, Molly, find us one.

Kathy McCullough

Scented Rectangles

Cut rectangles out of construction paper. Sprinkle a few drops of a flavored extract, such as vanilla, almond, lemon, and mint, on one of the rectangles. Repeat with different extracts on the remaining rectangles. Set out the rectangles and let your children take turns smelling them. When everyone has had a chance to smell all of the rectangles, cut the large rectangles into smaller ones for the children to take home.

Tasting

Rectangular Snack Mats

Select two rectangular items for snack, such as juice in a rectangular box and a rectangular graham cracker. Carefully trace around each item. Cut one set of these rectangles for each of your children. Give each child a sheet of construction paper and the two different sizes of rectangles. Let your children glue their rectangles on their construction paper any way they wish. Allow the glue to dry. Then give each child a box of juice and a graham cracker (or whatever food items you selected). Have the children place the items on the appropriate rectangles on their mats before eating them. Talk about the rectangular shapes as the children enjoy their snack.

Diamonds

Seeing

Find the Diamonds

On a sheet of paper, draw several large diamonds that overlap to make smaller diamonds (see illustration). Show the paper to your children. Ask them to look carefully at the paper and tell you how many diamonds are drawn on it. If necessary, point out the smaller diamonds made by the larger diamonds. Draw a different arrangement of diamonds on another sheet of paper and show it to the children. Ask them to count the diamonds again. Repeat as long as interest lasts.

Touching

Diamond Necklace

Cut diamond shapes out of sturdy paper. Punch a hole at the top of each shape. Bury three or four of the diamond shapes in your sandbox or in a dishpan full of sand. Have one of your children hunt for the paper diamonds as you sing the following song. As the child finds each diamond shape, help him or her string it on a length of yarn to make a necklace.

Sung to: "Clementine"

Found a diamond, found a diamond,

Found a diamond in the sand.

I think I'll make a necklace

With the diamond in my hand.

Jean Warren

Diamond Story

Give each of your children a paper diamond. Tell your children a story about diamonds. Ask the children to hold up their paper diamonds every time they hear you say the word *diamond*.

Smelling

Scented Kites

Cut diamond kite shapes out of construction paper. Set out the kite shapes and scented felt tip markers. Let your children use the markers to decorate the kites. Talk about the scents of the different markers. Which scents do they like the best? What will their kites smell like when they are finished? Hang the children's kites on the wall or a bulletin board at "nose" level, and add paper and yarn tails.

Tasting

Diamond Sandwiches

Prepare your children's favorite sandwiches for a snack or a meal. Remove the crusts from the sandwiches. Cut each whole sandwich into four triangles. Give each child at least two triangles. Help the children arrange the sandwich triangles on their plates to make diamond shapes.

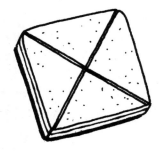
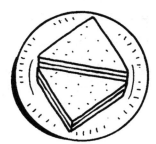

Hearts

Magic Hearts

For each of your children, use a black, nonpermanent felt tip marker to draw a large heart on a paper towel. Set out paintbrushes and cups of water. Show the children how to dip their brushes in the water and then over the heart drawing. Encourage them to watch how the colors in the black heart outline spread out.

Textured Hearts

Cut a large heart shape out of cardboard for each of your children. Set out a variety of textured materials, such as dried beans, rice, pasta, and fabric and ribbon scraps. Have the children glue the materials on their shapes to make Textured Hearts. Help them describe the different textures they have used.

Heart Hop

Place many heart stickers on the floor. Have your children gather around the hearts. Tell them that you are going to say the names of lots of shapes while they hop around, but whenever they hear *heart,* they should quickly hop to the closest heart on the floor and touch it (only one child per heart). When they hear the names of other shapes, they can begin hopping around again. Repeat as long as interest lasts.

Scented Hearts

Cut heart shapes out of sturdy paper. Collect two or three different spray bottles of cologne or perfume. Have your children sit in a circle. Carefully spray one of the scents into the air for the children to smell. Repeat with the other scents. Give each child one of the hearts. One at a time, have them come up and tell you which scent was their favorite. Then help them spray a little of that scent on their heart shapes.

Red Gelatin Hearts

Combine 1 cup unsweetened apple juice concentrate and 1 cup water in a saucepan and bring to a boil. In a separate bowl, empty 2 envelopes of unflavored gelatin and sprinkle on 1 teaspoon of unsweetened powdered raspberry drink mix. Add the heated liquid and stir until the gelatin is dissolved. Add 1 cup cold water. Pour mixture into a 9-by-13-inch baking pan that has been sprayed with nonstick cooking spray. Chill in the refrigerator. When the gelatin is set, use a heart-shaped cookie cutter to cut hearts out of the gelatin. Have your children describe how the hearts taste.

Stars

Night Sky Art

Use a white crayon to draw stars on white sheets of construction paper. Be sure to press down hard on the crayon while you are drawing. Give each of your children one of the sheets of paper. Set out paintbrushes and containers of diluted black or dark blue tempera paint. Let your children brush the diluted paint across their papers to make the crayon stars appear like stars in the night sky.

Touching

Reach for the Stars

Cut several star shapes out of heavy paper. Hang the stars so they are just out of reach of your children. You could hang them from the ceiling indoors, or from a tree branch or a clothesline outdoors. Invite your children to jump up and "reach for the stars" that hang above their heads. How many can they touch? Make the game more difficult by raising some of the stars up a little higher.

You're a Star

Give each of your children a star. It could be a star shape cut out of paper, a sticker star, or any other star that you have. Say the following rhyme, substituting the names of your children for those in the rhyme. Have the children listen carefully for their names. When they hear their names, have them hold up their stars.

Sung to: "Three Blind Mice"

I see stars, I see stars—

Lots of stars, lots of stars.

Katie's a star, and Joel's one, too,

Christina and Leia, to name a few.

Lorne's a star, and Meera's one, too.

I see stars.

Gayle Bittinger

Smelling

Scented Stars

Purchase a scented, yellow ink pad or make your own by adding lemon extract to yellow paint and pouring a small amount of the paint into a shallow container. Set out the ink pad and a rubber stamp or a sponge in the shape of a star. Let your children take turns stamping scented, yellow stars on sheets of paper.

Tasting

Star Soup

Let your children help you prepare a can of chicken and stars soup. Can they find the stars on the soup can label? Give each child a small bowl of soup. Have them find the star-shaped pasta in their soup before eating it.

Many Shapes

Art Shapes

For each of your children, cut a small shape out of a large sheet of paper. Ask the children to look at the holes in their papers and identify the shapes. Encourage the children to draw on their papers, incorporating the shape cutouts into their designs, if they wish.

Touching

Dough Shapes

Set out modeling dough and cookie cutters in the shapes your children have been learning about. Let the children practice making shapes out of the dough. Encourage them to figure out as many ways as they can to make shapes—rolling out the dough and cutting it with the cookie cutters, making shapes with their hands, and so on.

Matching Scents

Cut six different shapes out of heavy paper. Divide six cotton balls into three pairs. Sprinkle each pair of cotton balls with a different scent, such as lemon extract, vinegar, and a floral cologne. Glue one cotton ball on each shape. Let your children take turns sniffing the scented shapes and finding the matching scents. Ask them to name the shapes that have the same scents.

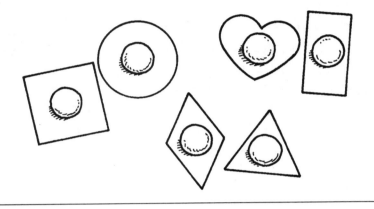

Tasting

Shape Sandwiches

Give each of your children a buttered slice of bread. Set out cookie cutters in familiar shapes. Let each child choose one of the cookie cutters to cut a shape out of his or her bread slice. Then give each child a second slice of buttered bread and a slice of cheese. Have the children put their sandwiches together with the cutout slices of bread on top to make Shape Sandwiches.

Hearing

Musical Shapes

Set out chairs, one for each of your children, in two rows back-to-back. Tape construction paper shapes to the chairs. Play some music and let the children walk around the chairs. Tell the children that when they hear the music stop, they will each need to find a chair to sit on. Stop the music and let each of them find a chair. To resume the game, call out shape names. When the children hear the name of the shape they're sitting on, have them stand up and get ready to walk around the chairs again. Continue as long as interest lasts.

One

Number One Book

Staple several sheets of paper together to make a book. On the cover of each book, write "My Number One Book" and one of your children's names. Give the children their books. Set out a variety of magazine picture cutouts. Make sure each cutout is a picture of just one thing, such as a dog, a cookie, a flower, or a child. Have the children select pictures for their books. Help them glue just one picture on each page. Let them read their Number One Books to you by looking at the pages and saying "one" and the name of the item, for example, "One dog. One cookie. One flower."

One for Each

Select a container with several compartments, such as an egg carton or a muffin tin. Set out the container and one small item for each compartment. Show your children how to put one item into each compartment, counting out "one" each time. Let the children take turns filling the compartments.

One Story

Collect a variety of story props and put them in a bag. Have your children sit in a circle. Take one item out of the bag and begin to tell a story about this one thing. Pass the bag around the circle and let your children take turns drawing an item out of the bag. Incorporate each item into your One Story. For example, if a teddy bear, a penny, and an apple were pulled out of the bag, in that order, your story could be, "One day, one bear went for a walk. On her walk she found one penny on the ground. She took her one penny to the store and bought one apple."

Smelling

One-Part Potpourri

Set out bowls with the following scented items: whole cloves, cinnamon sticks broken into small pieces, and dried orange peel. Put a small scoop into each bowl. Give each of your children a small resealable plastic bag. Tell them the "recipe" for this special potpourri: one scoop of each item. Let them take turns putting one scoop of each item into their bags. Help them seal their bags and attach a note saying, "In a small pan, put 1 tablespoon potpourri into 3 cups water and bring to a boil on top of the stove. Simmer, uncovered, to allow the spice scent to fill your home."

Tasting

One Snack

Serve your children one whole "some-thing" for snack. Choose an item that you might ordinarily serve in smaller pieces, such as an apple, a banana, or a graham cracker. Talk to the children about their One Snack as they enjoy eating it.

Two

Seeing

Two's a Pair

Cut large number 2 shapes out of
heavy paper. Set out glue and a collection of small objects, such as paper
clips, rubber bands, pasta shapes,
cotton balls, short yarn segments, and
dried beans. Let your children choose
pairs of the small objects and glue
them on their number 2 shapes.
Point out the shape of the number 2.
Encourage the children to count the
items in each pair.

Touching

Hunting for Twos

Cut out a variety of number 2s. You could cut them out of
magazines or newspapers (grocery ads are particularly
helpful) or cut the number 2 shape out of construction paper. Tape the numbers 2s all around your room. Invite your
children to join you on a "two hunt." Have them show you
their two hands. Ask them to look all around for the number 2. Each time they find the number, have them touch it
with their two hands.

Find a Partner

Have your children dance and move around while they listen to you say the names of numbers other than two. When they finally hear you say "Two," have them stop and quickly find a partner. Point out that each pair of children consists of only two children. Repeat the game as long as interest lasts.

Smelling

Smelling Cup Game

Collect five paper cups. Put cinnamon in one cup, mint extract in another, garlic in a third, and coffee grounds in two cups. Cover the cups with foil and fasten the foil to the cups with rubber bands. Carefully poke several holes in the foil on top of each cup. Show the cups to one of your children. Ask the child to sniff each cup. Which two cups match?

Hint: Make up several sets of five smelling cups, using scents you have readily available. Encourage your children to find the two matching cups in each set.

Tasting

Paired-Up Snacks

Serve foods that go together, such as crackers and cheese, apples and peanut butter, milk and cookies. Point out the two items that are being served. Encourage your children to think of other food pairs they enjoy eating.

Three

Three-Color Art

Set out three colors of art materials. For example, you could put out red, yellow, and blue paint; pink, purple, and green felt tip markers; or black, gold, and silver crayons. Give your children sheets of white paper. Let them create Three-Color Art with the materials available. Talk about the three colors they can see on their papers.

Touching

Touch a Three

Cut number 3 shapes out of various kinds of textured material, such as sandpaper, fake fur, felt, and cardboard. Let your children take turns using their hands and fingers to touch the number 3s. Help the children describe and name the various textures. Then have one child close his or her eyes. Give the child one of the shapes and ask the child to feel it carefully. What texture is it? Repeat for the other children.

Nursery Rhyme Fun

Invite your children to listen as you recite nursery rhymes with the number 3 in them, such as "Three Little Kittens," "Rub-a-Dub-Dub, Three Men in a Tub," "Baa, Baa, Black Sheep," and "Three Blind Mice." Talk about the three things in each rhyme.

Smelling

Three Flowers in a Row

Cut out a variety of flower shapes. Lightly spray the shapes with a floral-scented cologne. Give each child a sheet of construction paper with three green stems drawn on it. Have each child select three of the scented flower shapes to glue on top of the stems. Encourage the children to smell and count the flowers on their papers.

Tasting

Try Three

Serve your children a snack food that comes in three different varieties. For example, you could serve three different kinds of apples, cheeses, breads, crackers, or vegetables. Let the children tell you which ones they like the best.

Four

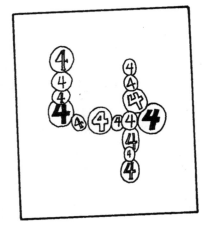

Number Collage

Set out a variety of grocery ads and other papers that have lots of numbers on them. Help your children look for and cut out the number 4s they find. When they have collected quite a few, let them glue their 4s on a large sheet of paper to make a number 4 collage.

Hint: If you wish, trace a large number 4 on the paper and have the children glue their cutout 4s along those lines.

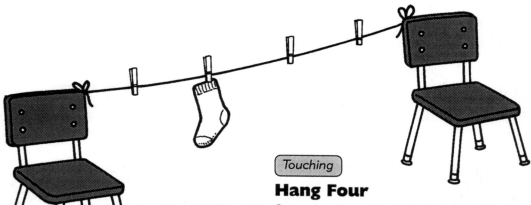

Hang Four

Stretch a length of clothesline between two chairs. Put four clothespins on the line. Set a basket of small clothing items beneath the clothesline. Invite one of your children to join you. Ask the child to hang up four items on the clothesline. Have the child count the items for you. Then give the child more specific directions. For example, you could ask the child to hang up four mittens, four blue socks, four scarves, and so on.

Four Little Stars

Cut four star shapes out of felt and place them on a flannelboard. Encourage your children to listen as you recite the following rhyme. Remove one star at a time, as indicated in the rhyme.

Four little stars winking at me.
One shot off, then there were three.

Three little stars with nothing to do.
One shot off, then there were two.

Two little stars afraid of the sun.
One shot off, then there was one.

One little star—alone is no fun.
It shot off, then there was none.

Jean Warren

Smelling

Four-Part Pudding

Prepare the following recipe ahead of time. Give each child a cup with a small amount of the pudding. Let the children smell the pudding and try to guess the four ingredients that went into it. Then let them eat their pudding. If you wish, let the children make their own batch of Four-Part Pudding to eat or share with others.

Pudding—Combine 3 ripe bananas, sliced; ½ cup unsweetened applesauce; 2 teaspoons peanut butter; and ¼ cup orange juice in a blender. Process until smooth.

Tasting

Snack Quarters

Serve your children a snack that can be divided into quarters, such as a piece of toast, a banana, a graham cracker, or a slice of cheese. Point out the four pieces on each child's plate. Does each piece taste the same as the others?

Five

Erase a Number

Write numbers all over a chalkboard, including many 5s. Show your children a number 5 that has been written on a sheet of paper and talk about the shape. Point to several of the number 5s on the chalkboard. Then give one of your children an eraser. Ask the child to erase one of the number 5s on the chalkboard and pass the eraser on to someone who has not yet had a turn. Repeat until each child has had a chance to erase a number 5.

Touching

Five Fingerprints

Set out construction paper and washable ink pads or paint pads. (To make your own paint pads, fold paper towels in half, place them in shallow containers, and pour on small amounts of paint.) Have your children hold up one hand. Count the five fingers on it. Show them how to press each finger on an ink pad or a paint pad, then on a sheet of paper to make fingerprints. Have them make a fingerprint for each finger. Together, count the fingerprints on their papers. Let them continue the fun by making as many fingerprints as they wish.

Extension: Encourage older children to position their fingerprints close together to make sets of five.

Give Me Five

Slowly beat a drum five times while your children count the beats with you. Repeat, beating the drum faster and faster. Have each child pretend his or her legs are a drum. Ask the children to beat their "drums" with you. Count out five beats at a time.

Extension: Let the children make their own drums out of boxes. Help the children write the number 5 on their drums.

I Like It

Prepare several smelling cups. (Directions can be found on page 45.) Have your children sit in a circle. Pass one of the smelling cups around the circle and let each child have a chance to sniff it. Ask the children who liked the scent to hold up five fingers. Repeat with the remaining smelling cups.

Five-Fruit Salad

Let your children help you select five fruits to be put into a fruit salad. Have them help you wash and prepare the fruits. Put the fruit in a bowl. Give each child a small serving of the Five-Fruit Salad to eat. How do they like the taste of salad? Which fruit do they think tastes the best?

Many Numbers

Counting Holes

Select five index cards. On the left-hand side of each card, write a number from 1 to 5. On the right-hand side, punch a matching number of holes with a hole punch. Let your children take turns counting the number of holes in the cards and naming the matching numbers.

Touching

Stack a Tower

Number five index cards from 1 to 5 with numbers and dots. Set out the cards along with 15 blocks. Show your children how to select one of the cards, count the dots, then build a tower with the same number of blocks. Repeat with the remaining cards. Let your children take turns playing this stacking game.

Hearing

Robot Game

Ask your children to pretend to be robots that can only move when they hear beeps. Tell them that one beep means move forward, and two beeps mean stop. Begin beeping. As your children catch on to this game, add more commands. For example, three beeps could mean go backward and four beeps could mean turn around.

Smelling

The Children's Graph

Set up several chairs a few feet apart, and place a different smelling cup on each one. (Directions for making smelling cups can be found on page 45.) One at a time, invite your children to sniff the contents of each cup and stand behind the chair holding the scent they like the best. When everyone has had a turn, count the children standing behind each chair. Which scent was the most popular? Which was the least? Point out that by standing like this, they have made a graph with their bodies.

Tasting

Salad Bar

Prepare a variety of ingredients for a salad bar. On a sheet of plain paper, draw a simple picture of each of the ingredients. Make a photocopy of this paper for each child. Tell your children that they will be making their own salads, following their own recipes. Work with each child to make a recipe for his or her salad. Have the children tell you how many spoonfuls of each item they want in their salads. Write the number by each item. (It is okay for an item to have a zero.) Let the children prepare their salads, following their recipes.

Big and Little

Printing Fun

Collect rubber stamps in big and little sizes. Set out the stamps and several washable ink pads. Cut some construction paper into quarters to make little sheets of paper and leave other construction paper whole for big sheets. Let your children use the rubber stamps to make prints on the big and little papers in any way they wish. Then have them use the big rubber stamps to stamp big prints on the big sheets of paper, and the little rubber stamps to stamp little prints on the little sheets.

Touching

Then and Now

Set out several articles of baby clothes (pants, shirt, socks, hat, etc.). Find the same articles of clothing in preschooler size. Mix up the clothes and place them in a basket. Let your children take turns sorting the items. Encourage them to compare the sizes. Let them try on a baby's hat or sock. Why don't these clothes fit anymore? Talk about what your children were like when they were little and wore baby clothes. What things can they do now that they are big?

Big Bear, Little Bear

Sing the following song with your children. As they listen to the words, have them pretend to be Big Bear or Little Bear and move around the room.

Sung to: "London Bridge"

Here comes Big Bear,

Stomp, stomp, stomp,

Stomp, stomp, stomp,

Stomp, stomp, stomp.

Here comes Big Bear,

Stomp, stomp, stomp,

Stomp, stomp, Big Bear.

Here comes Little Bear,

Tip, tap, tip,

Tip, tap, tip,

Tip, tap, tip.

Here comes Little Bear,

Tip, tap, tip,

Tip, tap, Little Bear.

Elizabeth McKinnon

Smelling

Big and Little Scents

Make up several smelling cups, using some big cups and some little cups. (Directions for making the smelling cups can be found on page 45.) Put a different scent in each cup. Ask one of your children to sniff one of the big cups. What's in it? Invite another child to come up and smell one of the little cups. Hold out a big smelling cup and a little smelling cup. Ask a child to come up and smell both. Which one smells the best, the big or the little cup?

Tasting

Just What I Wanted

Prepare a snack food that can be served easily in big and little quantities, such as cottage cheese, gelatin, or yogurt. As you serve the food to your children, ask them to tell you if they would like a big or little helping.

Stop and Go

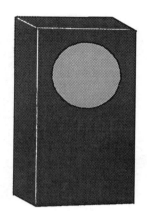

Seeing

Traffic Signal Game

Make a simple traffic signal by covering a half-gallon milk carton with black construction paper. On one side, attach a red circle near the top of the carton. On the opposite side, attach a green circle near the bottom of the carton. Show your children the red circle on the carton. Tell them that when they see this, they should say "Stop!" Show the green circle and ask them to say "Go!" whenever they see it. Spin the signal around and let the children play the game.

Touching

Fingerpainting Fun

Have your children sit around a washable table. Place a small dollop of fingerpaint in front of each child. Tell your children that when you say "Go," they may fingerpaint on the table however they wish. When you say "Stop," they must lift their hands off the table. Repeat as often as you like. Before the final "stop," tell the children that you will be making prints of their final finger-painting designs. To make prints, carefully place a sheet of paper over each child's work and rub gently. The design will transfer to the paper.

Stop and Go Scents

Prepare several smelling cups. (See page 45 for directions for making smelling cups, if needed.) Sit down with one of your children. Tell the child to say "Go" when he or she is ready to smell one of the cups, and "Stop" when he or she is finished. Let the child smell all of the cups using this technique. Which one smelled the best?

Variation: Divide older children into pairs and let them take turns holding up the cups and sniffing them.

Hearing

Traffic Light Song

Sing the following song with your children. Have them act out the motions as indicated in the song.

Sung to: "Twinkle, Twinkle, Little Star"

Twinkle, twinkle, traffic light,
  (Open and close fingers quickly.)

Shining brightly day and night.

When it's green, we can go.
  (Walk forward.)

When it's red, we stop, you know.
  (Stop walking.)

Twinkle, twinkle, traffic light,
  (Open and close fingers quickly.)

Shining brightly day and night.

Judith McNitt

Tasting

How Much?

Prepare a snack such as pretzels or popcorn. Give each of your children small bowls. Stand beside one of your children. Begin scooping out the snack when the child says "Go." Stop filling the child's bowl when he or she says "Stop."

Hot and Cold

Is It Hot or Cold?

Cut out magazine pictures of things that are hot (a bowl of soup, the sun, a cup of coffee, etc.) and things that are cold (ice cream, snow, ice, etc.). Have your children look at each picture and decide if the object shown is hot or cold.

Touching

To the Touch

Bring in a hair dryer and a heating pad. (A hot water bottle works well, too.) Turn them on and let your children feel the warm air from the hair dryer and the warmth of the heating pad. (Close supervision is necessary when any appliance is used by or near children.) Then set out a tray of ice cubes and a bowl of ice water for the children to touch. Which ones feels best?

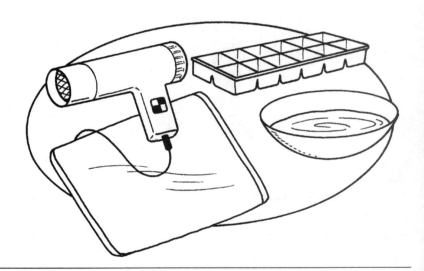

Hearing

Hot or Cold Game

Have your children sit in a circle. Explain to them that you will be describing different places. If it is a place that sounds like it is hot, have them fan themselves with their hands. If it is a place that sounds cold, have them wrap their arms around themselves and shiver. Some examples include, "I'm on a beach, the sun is shining, and I'm walking barefoot;" or, "The wind is blowing and there's snow on the ground."

Warm It Up

Fill a crockpot with water and place some potpourri in it. Before turning on the crockpot, invite your children to come and smell the potpourri. When the water and potpourri are cold, how close do they have to be to smell it? Now turn on the crockpot and let the potpourri smell waft through the room. Encourage your children to use their noses to notice the nice smell everywhere. Explain that when the potpourri and water are heated, the scent floats into the air and drifts around.

Hot and Cold Snack

Let your children help you make hot cocoa. Give each child a cup of cocoa and a spoon. Have them taste the cocoa. Is it hot or cold? Now spray a small amount of whipping cream on top of each child's cocoa. Is the cream hot or cold? Let the children enjoy their hot cocoa and cold whipping cream together.

On and Off

Chalkboard Art

Set out a chalkboard, chalk, and an eraser. Let your children take turns drawing on the chalkboard with the chalk and using the eraser to wipe off their drawings. Ask older children to follow directions such as, "Draw two lines on the chalkboard. Wipe off one line."

Touching

On and Off Board

Collect a nonaluminum baking sheet and several magnets. Let your children take turns putting the magnets on and off the baking sheet. Help them notice the position of the magnets. For example, say, "The red magnet is off the board. The blue magnet is on it."

Hearing

Hat Game

Sing the following song to your children. As they listen to the words of the song, let them use real or pretend hats to act out the motions.

Sung to: "The Farmer in the Dell"

I put my hat on.

I take my hat off.

I put my hat right on my head,

And then I take it off.

Gayle Bittinger

Turn Off Your Nose

Have your children sit in a circle. Tell them they can turn "off" their sense of smell by holding their nostrils closed. Let them practice this. Put a strong-smelling food, such as a cut onion, in the middle of the circle. Make sure that everyone can smell it. Now, have the children turn off the smell by plugging their nose. How does it work? Can they turn "on" their sense of smell? Set out a sliced banana and let them try.

Tasting

On and Off Snack

Arrange a simple snack food, such as crackers, on a platter. Give each of your children a plate or a napkin. Pass the platter around to the children saying, "Please take some crackers off my platter and place them on your plate." Emphasize "off" and "on" with each child. Encourage the children to tell you how many crackers they have put on their plates.

In and Out

Pop-Out Puppet

Draw a puppet face on the end of a craft stick. Cut a slit in the bottom of a paper cup. Slide the craft stick through the slit to make a handle. Hold onto the handle to make the puppet move up and down, so it appears to be popping out of the cup and jumping back in the cup. Have your children watch the puppet and tell you when it is in the cup and when it has popped out of the cup.

Touching

Roll in the Box

Collect a small rubber ball and a shoebox with a lid . Cut a hole in the lid of the shoebox large enough for the ball to fit through. Cut a hole large enough for a child's hand in the side of the box. Tape the lid upside down on top of the shoebox. Place the rubber ball on top of the lid. Let your children take turns moving the box around to make the ball fall into the hole. Show them how to get the ball out of the box by reaching in the side.

In and Out Game

Give each of your children a paper cup and five cotton balls. Have the children listen carefully as you give them directions such as, "Put two cotton balls in the cup. Take out one cotton ball. Put in two more cotton balls. Take out three cotton balls." As your children become more experienced with this game, let them take turns giving the directions.

 Smelling

Smelling Tent

Drape a sheet over a table to make a tent in your room. Put several scented sachets in the tent. Let your children go into the tent two or three at a time, to sniff the sachets. When they are finished, have them come out of the tent and select other children to go in. Leave the tent up for a while and let the children go in and out of it when they wish.

Tasting

Cereal Mix

Set out several different bowls of cereal. Give each of your children a bowl and a spoon. Let the children spoon a little of each cereal into their bowls. Help them pour milk in their bowls, too. Then let them take their cereal out, one spoonful at a time, and eat it.

Over and Under

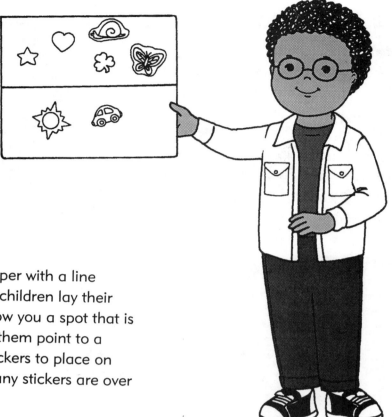

Sticker Picture

Give each of your children a sheet of paper with a line drawn across the middle of it. Have the children lay their papers in front of them. Ask them to show you a spot that is over the line on their papers, then have them point to a spot under the line. Give the children stickers to place on their papers. Have them tell you how many stickers are over the line and how many are under it.

Touching

Over and Under the Bridge

Make a toy bridge for your children's toy cars. (Use blocks, boxes, or whatever you have handy.) When the bridge is complete, let your children play with it. Encourage them to drive their cars over and under the bridge.

Movement Game

Tell your children to listen carefully to the directions and to move their bodies accordingly. Try directions such as, "Put your hands over your head. Put your arms under your knees. Put your hands over your nose. Put your feet over your head."

Over and Under Snacktime

Instead of sitting at a table for snack, have the children find places around the room to sit—places that are over or under something. As you take the children their snacks, have them tell you what they are sitting over or under. Let them eat their snacks right where they are, over and under.

Smelling

Find the Scents

Prepare several different smelling cups. (See page 45 for directions, if needed.) Place the cups around the room in places that are over or under something else. Let your children look all around for the cups. Have them sniff the cups and then put them back where they were. As they are exploring, ask them to tell you what they smell under the table, over the blocks, under the chair, over the crayons, and so on.

First and Last

Look and Tell

Select three flannelboard shapes that your children are familiar with and place them on a flannelboard, one at a time, in a line. Point out which flannelboard shape was first in the line, and which one was last. Take the shapes off and put them on again in a different order. Let the children tell you which one was first and which one was last. Repeat as long as interest lasts.

Touching

Arranging Stuffies

Set out several different stuffed animals, such as a teddy bear, a kitty cat, and a monkey. Ask one of your children to arrange them in a line, with the teddy bear first and the kitty cat last. Then ask the child to rearrange them and tell you which is first and which is last.

Hearing

What Comes First?

Ask your children to listen carefully and to put on their thinking caps. Explain that you will name two things that they do. You want them to tell you which of those two activities has to be done first, for example, "What comes first, putting on your coat or putting on your clothes? Playing with your toys or putting them away? Getting in bed or putting on pajamas?"

First and Last Scents

Prepare two smelling cups. (Directions for making the smelling cups can be found on page 45.) Set the cups on a table. Let your children sit, one at a time, in front of the cups. Ask them to decide which cup they will smell first and which one they will smell last. After both cups have been sniffed, have the children tell you which one they liked best, the first or the last.

Tasting

Snacktime Fun

Tell your children which snack foods you have prepared today. Have them guess which food you will be serving first, then serve the food. Continue serving the prepared snacks until just before the last one. Ask the children to guess what the last food will be. Did they remember? Serve the last snack food to your children.

Heavy and Light

Seeing

Heavy and Light Collage

Collect a variety of heavy collage materials (wood scraps, small pebbles, old nuts and bolts, etc.) and light collage materials (feathers, fabric scraps, paper shapes, etc.). Set out sheets of cardboard or heavy paper and glue. Let the children select several heavy and light items to glue onto their cardboard to make collages.

Touching

I Can Lift That

Collect a variety of heavy objects and light objects. Place them together in a box. Let your children, one a time, reach into the box, lift out one of the objects and say if it is heavy or light. Have them put the heavy objects in one pile and the light objects in another. Can the children think of other things, both heavy and light, to add to the piles?

Fruit Scents

Purchase several different fruits at the grocery store, including a heavy watermelon and light grapes. Arrange the fruits on a table. Prepare them so that the scent of each one can be easily smelled. Let the children pick up the fruits. Which one is the heaviest? What does it smell like? Which fruit is the lightest? How does it smell? Set out just two fruits. Ask one of the children to tell you which is the heaviest. Of those two, which one smells best, the heavy fruit or the light fruit?

Here's Something Heavy

Set out a heavy book, a heavy rock, a light feather, and a light scarf. Ask your children to sit around the objects. Give your children directions using the words *heavy* and *light*, for example, "Pick up an item that's light. Give a heavy object to Kara. Balance a light object on your head." Can they tell by looking whether something is heavy or light?

Heavy and Light Snacks

Set out two identical bowls. Fill one bowl with apple slices and the other with popcorn. Let the children take turns holding the bowls. Which is lightest? Which is heaviest? Give each child a small amount of each snack food, heavy and light.

High and Low

Seeing

Water Designs

Fill spray bottles with water. Let your children take the bottles outside and use them to spray water on a wall. Encourage them to spray way up high and way down low. What do their high and low designs look like? Have them point to water that's been sprayed low and water that's been sprayed high.

Touching

High and Low Toys

Invite your children to help you rearrange the items in a two-shelf bookcase or toy cabinet. As you are working, say such things as, "Put the bunny book on the high shelf. Put the plastic dinosaurs on the low shelf. Move the teddy bear to the low shelf so we can put the ball next to it."

Hearing

Music, Music, Music

Let your children help you choose a favorite song. Together, sing the song first in high voices, then in low voices. Continue by playing sets of high and low notes on a piano, a xylophone, or another instrument. Have your children stretch their hands up high when they hear a high note and reach them down low when they hear a low note.

Sniffing High and Low

Cut a sheet of construction paper into 2-inch strips. Tape enough strips together to make a 3-foot-long strip. Put a drop of vanilla extract at the top of the strip and a drop of peppermint extract at the bottom of the strip. Attach the strip to a wall. Ask your children if they can discover which scent is up high on the strip and which one is down low. Encourage them to think of ways to smell up high (jump, stand on a stool, ask a tall person, etc.). Which scent did they like the best, high or low?

Where Do You Eat Your Food?

Have your children pretend to be giraffes. Ask them if giraffes eat food that is down low or up high. Offer them lettuce leaves and have them pretend to be giraffes eating the leaves from their high trees. Then have your children pretend to be rabbits. Ask them if rabbits eat food that is up high or down low. Give the children carrot sticks to nibble on like rabbits. Let your children think of other animals that eat their meals up high or down low.

New Year's Day

Party Hats

Make cone-shaped hats out of construction paper for your children. Set out a variety of decorating materials, such as crepe paper, paper scraps, sequins, stickers, and felt tip markers. Invite the children to arrange the materials on their hats until they look just right and then glue them in place. When they are finished, attach two yarn ties to the sides of each child's hat. Help the children put on their hats, and have a mirror available so they can see the results. Let the children wear their hats while they celebrate the new year.

Touching

Party Basket

Collect a variety of items you might need to celebrate the new year (party hat, noisemaker, streamer, etc.). Place all of the items in a bag. Let your children take turns reaching into the bag and identifying the objects by touch.

New Year's Parade

Let your children ring in the new year with a parade. First, have the children make noisemakers. Give each child two plain paper cups. Let the children decorate their cups with crayons or felt tip markers. When each child is finished, put a scoop of dried beans or rice in one of his or her cups and securely tape the other cup on top, rim to rim. Have the children hold onto their noisemakers and wear their hats from the Party Hats activity on the opposite page. Let the children march around the room, celebrating the new year.

Smelling

Nuts and Bolts Snack Mix

Let your children help you make this snack mix for their New Year's celebration. Encourage them to smell the ingredients before and after they are mixed together.

    4 cups bite-size shredded wheat

  ⅓ cup margarine, melted

    Garlic powder

1½ cups stick pretzels, broken in half

  ½ cup dry-roasted peanuts

  ½ cup raisins

Spread out shredded wheat on a baking pan. Drizzle with melted margarine and sprinkle on garlic powder to taste. Bake at 350°F for 15 minutes. Add pretzel sticks, peanuts, and raisins. Store in an airtight container.

Tasting

Party Treats

Let your children help you prepare a simple party menu. Serve juice, pretzels, veggies, and cheese cubes. Have the children taste each of the items from the menu. Which ones do they like the best? If they were planning a party, which foods would they like to serve?

Martin Luther King Jr. Day

Seeing

Friendship Wreath

Set out construction paper in a variety of skin tones. Have each of your children select one of the papers. Help the children trace around one of their hands and cut out the tracing. On a large sheet of butcher paper, draw a large circle. Place the butcher paper on a table or the floor. One at a time, have the children attach their paper hand shapes to the circle, fingers and wrists overlapping. When everyone's hand is on the wreath, talk about all the different colors. Ask the children to think of ways we can all help each other and give each other a hand.

Touching

Follow the Leader

Have your children stand in a line, shoulder to shoulder, and hold hands. Have the first child in the line start the group on a walk. Tell your children that they need to hold hands very carefully and must be sure not to pull or tug on others. Help the leader notice when to slow down to keep the group together, and when to go ahead. Let the children take turns being the leader. You may wish to organize several groups of three or four children, instead of having one large group.

Talking Tube

Decorate a toilet tissue tube. Show the tube to your children. Explain that when someone has the tube, only that person may talk—everyone else must listen. Ask them to think about ways they care for each other. Give the tube to a child. Have that child tell you a way to care for someone else, then pass the tube to a child who has not had a turn. Continue until everyone has had a turn.

Smelling

Partner Game

Talk with your children about the way Martin Luther King Jr. encouraged cooperation. Ask them to practice cooperation as they explore the scents in this activity. Prepare several smelling cups. (See page 45 for directions for making smelling cups.) Invite two children to sit at a table to smell the cups. Have the children work together to decide who will smell which cup first, and so on. Encourage them to talk to each other and to work out any problems.

Tasting

Snack Buddies

Have your children pair up at snacktime. Ask each pair to find a different place to eat in the room. Pass out an easy "no-spill" snack. Let the children eat their snacks and visit with their partners. Have each pair wait until both of them have finished with snack before cleaning up.

Groundhog Day

Seeing

Groundhog Game

Find a very bright light that casts shadows when it is turned on. (A lamp without a shade works well.) Dim the lights in your room. Talk about Groundhog Day with your children. Tell them that if the groundhog sees its shadow, it jumps back inside its hole and hides for six more weeks of winter. But if it doesn't see its shadow, it comes out to play because it will be spring soon. Have the children pretend to be groundhogs. Ask them to curl up on the floor and hide their heads. Turn on the bright light and have the groundhogs wake up. Since they see their shadow, have them curl up on the floor again. Repeat the game, this time turning the bright light off. When the groundhogs don't see their shadows, let them come out to play. Repeat the game as long as interest lasts.

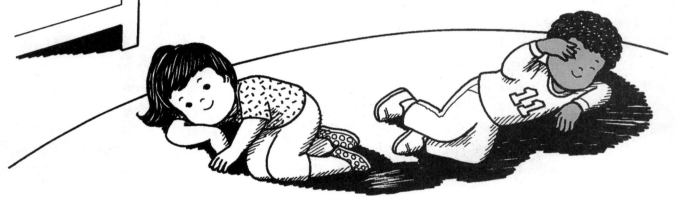

Touching

Shadow Touch

Play this game outside on a sunny day. Have your children find their shadows. Point out how their shadows move with them. Encourage them to find ways to make their shadows "touch" other things, such as playground equipment, a building, the sandbox, a person, even another shadow.

Spring and Winter

Cut out magazine pictures that show scenes of spring and scenes of winter. Let each of your children glue a spring picture to the front of a paper plate and a winter picture to the back. Let the children hold their paper plates. When you say "spring," have the children hold up the spring sides of their plates. When you say "winter," have them hold up the winter sides.

Spring Scents

Bring in several different kinds of spring flowers arranged in a sturdy vase. Place the vase on a table. Talk with your children about how these flowers are a sign that spring is on its way. Let the children pretend to be groundhogs that have not seen their shadows, looking for signs of spring. Have them take turns sniffing the flowers in the vase.

Groundhog Lunch

Groundhogs like to nibble on grasses and other greens that grow near their burrows. For Groundhog Lunches, let your children help make watercress and romaine lettuce salads to eat with a favorite dressing.

Valentine's Day

Seeing

Seeing Hearts

Cut heart shapes out of construction paper, then cut each heart shape in half. Set out the heart halves and small, rectangular mirrors. Invite a few of your children to join you. Challenge them to find a way to use the heart halves and mirrors to create whole hearts. If needed, show them how to hold a mirror along the cut side of a heart to do this.

Touching

Sending Valentines

Fold and trim red, pink, and white construction paper to make cards that will fit inside envelopes. Let your children decorate the cards for their parents. Put each child's card into an envelope and address it to the child's family. Help the children put stamps on their envelopes. Take the children to a mailbox and let them mail their valentines.

The Roberts Family
55 Willow Way
Springfield, USA
62555

U.S. MAIL

Color Valentines

Give each of your children a red, blue, pink, yellow, or green valentine heart. Say the following rhyme, and have the children listen carefully. When they hear the color of their valentine, have them hold it up in the air.

Valentines red,

Valentines blue,

Valentines pink

Say "I love you."

Valentines yellow,

Valentines green,

Prettiest valentines

I've ever seen!

Jean Warren

Smelling

Box of Chocolate

Purchase a heart-shaped box of chocolates. Show your children the box. Ask them if they can guess what's inside. Have them close their eyes. Open the box and let each child sniff the chocolate. Now can they guess what's inside? If you wish, let each child have one of the chocolates at snacktime.

Tasting

Heart Sandwiches

Use a cookie cutter to cut heart shapes out of bread, lunch meat, and cheese slices. Give each of your children the sandwich fixings on a plate. Let the children put their sandwiches together before eating them.

St. Patrick's Day

Seeing

Magic Pudding

For each of your children, place 1 table-spoon instant pistachio pudding mix in a baby food jar. Add 2 tablespoons cold milk and watch as the contents turn green. Put lids securely on the jars and have the children shake them for about 45 seconds. Then let the children eat their pudding snacks with small spoons.

Touching

Weighing Gold

Collect rocks in a variety of sizes and spray-paint them gold. Set out the nuggets of "gold" and a scale. Let your children weigh the gold. How much do four nuggets of gold weigh? How many nuggets of gold does it take to make three pounds? Encourage the children to find additional ways to weigh the gold nuggets.

Hearing

Hot and Cold

Borrow some of the gold nuggets from the Weighing Gold activity on this page and put them into a pot. Hide the pot of gold somewhere in your room. Ask one of your children to find the pot. Tell the child that you will say "hot" when he or she is getting closer to the pot of gold, and "cold" when he or she is getting farther away. After the child has found the pot of gold, let him or her hide it for the next child. Depending on the age and skill of your children, you may wish to let them give the hot and cold directions.

Leprechaun Treats

Purchase ready-made cookie dough from your grocery store's refrigerator section (or use your favorite homemade cookie dough). Let your children help you scoop or slice the dough onto baking sheets. Bake the cookies according to the directions on the package. As the cookies are baking, encourage your children to notice the way they smell. Do the children like the smell? When the cookies are done, put several of them on a plate to be left out for the leprechauns. Let each child have one of the remaining cookies. Do the cookies taste like they smell? When the children are away, "eat" the leprechaun cookies. You could also leave a note thanking the children and telling them that the delicious smell of the cookies brought you to their room.

Tasting

Irish Soda Bread

Let your children help you make this tasty Irish treat.

- 2 cups all-purpose flour, sifted
- 1 Tbsp. baking soda
- ½ tsp. salt
- ¼ cup butter or margarine
- 1 cup milk
- ½ cup raisins or currants

In a large bowl, mix the flour, soda, and salt together. Use fingers to blend in butter. Stir in milk and add raisins or currants. Knead the dough briefly, then shape into a flat loaf and place in a greased pie tin. Bake at 350°F for 30 to 35 minutes. Cut into wedges and serve warm with butter.

Easter

Tissue Eggs

Set out plastic eggs, brushes, a mixture of one part glue and one part water, and small pieces of tissue paper. Let your children brush the eggs with the glue mixture and put the tissue paper over the glue, adding more of the glue mixture as needed. Let the eggs dry. If you wish, have the children add a second layer of the glue mixture and tissue paper. When the eggs are dry, spray them with a clear shellac in an area away from the children. Encourage the children to look carefully at their finished eggs. What colors can they see on their eggs? Can they see places where colors blended together to make new colors?

Touching

Egg Hunt

For each of your children, prepare a treasure hunt by tying a small treasure to the end of a length of yarn and placing the treasure inside of a plastic egg with the yarn hanging out. Hide the eggs in your room and weave the remaining yarn lengths all around. Be sure to go over, under, and around as many things as possible. Give each child one of the loose ends of yarn. Have the children follow their yarn to their treasure egg.

Bunny Jump

Have your children pretend to be Easter bunnies, hopping outside in the sunshine. After a few minutes' practice being a bunny, ask one child to be the leader and call out the following phrase, "Bunnies, jump _____ times," while the other children listen. Have the child fill in the blank with a number from 1 to 10. Count together as the bunnies jump. Let each child have a chance to be the leader.

Smelling

Smelling Baskets

Make three smelling cups, each with a different scent. (See page 45 for directions.) Place each cup in a different Easter basket. Let your children take turns sniffing the scent in each basket. Give each child a plastic Easter egg to place in the basket with his or her favorite scent. When all of the eggs have been placed, look at the "basket graph" with the children. Which scent was the most popular? Which was the least?

Tasting

Jelly Bean Tasting

Give each of your children a napkin with three or four jelly beans in different flavors on it. Let the children taste each flavor of jelly bean separately. Which one did they like the best? If you wish, make a graph that shows how many children preferred each flavor.

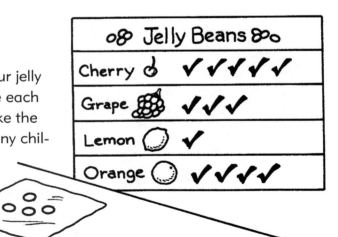

oꝗ Jelly Beans ꝗo	
Cherry 🍒	✓ ✓ ✓ ✓ ✓
Grape 🍇	✓ ✓ ✓
Lemon 🍋	✓
Orange 🍊	✓ ✓ ✓ ✓

May Day

Seeing

May Baskets

Give your children paper doilies to use in making simple May Baskets. Cut small squares from a variety of colors of tissue paper. Let the children brush glue on the centers of their doilies. Then have them crumple the tissue paper squares and place them on top of the glue for flowers. Attach a ribbon or yarn handle to opposite sides of each doily. When the children hold onto the handles, the sides of the doilies curl up, turning the doilies into flower-filled baskets.

Touching

Counting Flowers

Prepare five May Day baskets. (Margarine tubs covered with construction paper work well). Number the baskets from 1 to 5. Set out the baskets and 15 silk or plastic flowers. (Real flowers also work.) Let the children take turns putting the appropriate number of flowers into each basket.

I Made a Basket

Sing the following song with your children and have them act out the motions. Talk about the tradition of hanging May Day baskets on doors to surprise and treat neighbors.

Sung to: "Twinkle, Twinkle, Little Star"

May Day, May Day, how do you do?

I made a basket just for you.
(Hand someone a pretend basket.)

May Day, May Day, I made one more.

I will hang it on a door.
(Pretend to hang basket.)

Knock, knock, knock; run, run, run—
(Make knocking motions, then run in place.)

May Day is a lot of fun!

Kristine Wagoner

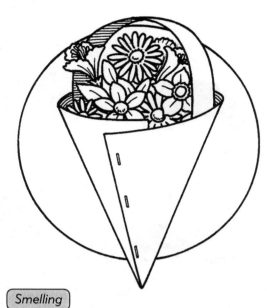

Smelling

May Day Basket

Let your children help you make a basket for May Day, using flowers with as many different scents as possible. Invite each child to bring in a flower. Take turns smelling each other's flowers. Have the children place the flowers in the basket you provide. Let them help you secretly deliver the basket to another group, one of your helpers, or a neighbor.

Tasting

May Day Snack Baskets

Let your children decorate paper cups using flower stickers or flower pictures cut from wrapping paper or seed catalogs. Attach pipe cleaner handles to the cups to make baskets. At snacktime, tuck a square of waxed paper inside each basket. Add small pieces of fresh fruit for "flowers."

Fourth of July

Packed for a Picnic

On a tray, place items you might need for a picnic. Show the items to your children. Hide the tray and remove one of the items. Show the children the tray again. Have them look carefully at the items and guess which one is missing. Repeat as long as interest lasts. To make the game a little harder, take away more than one item at a time.

Touching

Painted Fireworks

Give each of your children a square of butcher paper or fingerpaint paper with a dollop of fingerpaint on it. Ask your children to think about fireworks exploding in the air. Have them pretend their fingers are the fireworks, popping up and slowly falling down in arcs to create beautiful designs in their fingerpaint.

Fireworks Popping

Let your children pretend to be fireworks. When you say "Boom," have everyone start making fireworks sounds and moving around like fireworks. (You can eliminate the sound part, if you wish.) Have them stop and drop to the floor when they hear you say, "Crash!"

Smelling

Lemonade Scents

Set out the ingredients for lemonade: 4 lemons, cut in half; 3 cups water; and ½ cup sugar. Let your children smell each of the ingredients. Help the children squeeze the juice out of the lemons. Put the lemon juice in a pitcher, along with the water and sugar. Stir well. Give each child a small taste of lemonade. How does it smell? Can they smell the lemons? The water? The sugar? Let the children enjoy the lemonade at their Fourth of July Picnic.

Tasting

Fourth of July Picnic

Let your children help you plan a picnic for the Fourth of July. Talk about the kinds of foods people enjoy eating at picnics. Select a few to put on your menu, including the lemonade from the Lemonade Scents activity on this page. On the day of the picnic, let the children help you prepare the food and set the table, then enjoy your picnic together.

Halloween

Seeing

Costume Surprise

Tack up one or more child-size costumes, such as a clown and a firefighter, onto a wall or door so that the feet of the costume just brush the floor. Put a mirror where the child's face would fit in the costume. When your children look at the costumes, they'll see themselves dressed up. (*Note:* Please do not use scary costumes with young children, especially with this mirror technique. Young children can become very upset and fearful.)

Touching

Jack-O'-Lantern Fun

Cut pumpkin shapes from orange construction paper. Let your children use geometric-shaped rubber stamps (circles, triangles, squares, etc.) and a black ink pad to add a face to each pumpkin. Encourage them to experiment with different ways of arranging the rubber stamp prints to make different faces.

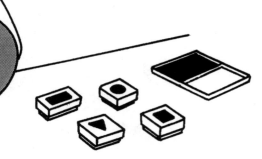

Halloween Pantomime

Put on some Halloween music and let your children act out various movements as you name them. For example, ask the children to fly like bats, walk like monsters, or creep like cats.

Smelling

Mini-Jack-O'-Lanterns

Provide one orange or tangerine and a handful of cloves for each of your children. (Cloves are often available less expensively in bulk.) Show the children how to poke the sharp ends of the cloves into their oranges to form a jack-o'-lantern face.

Tasting

Halloween Snack

Prepare a Halloween brew by combining 2 cups apple juice, ½ cup orange juice, 1 cinnamon stick, and 2 whole cloves in a saucepan. Simmer for 20 to 30 minutes. Let cool slightly and remove the cinnamon stick and cloves before pouring into cups. Wash and dry a large plastic jack-o'-lantern. Fill the jack-o'-lantern with pretzels. Let each of your children take a handful of pretzels out of the jack-o'-lantern to enjoy with their Halloween brew.

Thanksgiving

Seeing

Guessing Game

On a sheet of construction paper, glue a magazine picture of a favorite Thanksgiving food. Place a plain sheet of construction paper over the picture and staple it in place on the left-hand side. Cut the top sheet of construction paper horizontally into four sections. Show the covered picture to your children. Fold back one of the sections. Have the children look carefully at the part of the picture they can see and try to guess what food it is. Keep folding back sections until the children guess what the food is. Repeat with as many different Thanksgiving foods as you like.

Touching

Pin the Feathers

Cut a turkey shape (minus the feathers) out of brown construction paper. Tape the turkey shape to a wall at your children's eye level. Give each of your children a colorful feather with a loop of tape attached to the back. (Colorful feathers are available at craft stores.) Let the children take turns putting the feathers on the turkey. Depending on the ages of your children, you may wish to have them wear a blindfold, have them close their eyes, or spin them before they walk to the turkey.

Riddle Game

Make up riddles about fruits and vegetables or other foods that could be on a Thanksgiving table. Have your children listen carefully and try to guess which food you are talking about.

Cornucopia

Fill a cornucopia with veggies, such as carrot sticks, celery sticks, red pepper strips, broccoli flowerets, and cucumber coins. Have your children help you make a simple vegetable dip. Let the children select vegetables from the cornucopia to place on their plates, serve themselves a small scoop of dip, and enjoy all the different tastes.

Smelling

Smells So Good

Select a favorite Thanksgiving dish to prepare with your children. Have the children smell the ingredients as they are put together. Encourage them to smell the dish while it is cooking, too. When the dish is ready, serve each child a small portion. Have them smell the food before eating it. How do all the different smells compare? Which one do they like best?

Hanukkah

Seeing

Hanukkah Candles

Set out brushes and tempera paint.
Let each of your children paint a cardboard toilet tissue tube to look like a
candle. (Be sure to make one for yourself as well.) When the paint is dry,
give each child a craft stick with a
yellow construction paper flame shape
glued to the top. Show the children
how to "light" their candle puppets
by pushing their craft stick flames up
through their painted tubes. Now have
the children watch you carefully. When
you light your candle, have them light
theirs. When you put out your candle,
have them put out theirs.

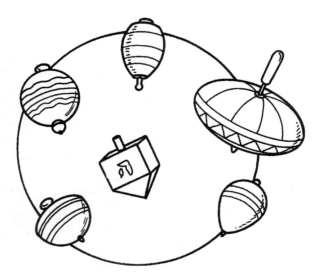

Touching

Spin the Top

Set out an assortment of tops, including a dreidel. Let your children practice spinning the tops. Which one is
the easiest to spin? Which one is the
hardest? Which top can spin the
longest?

Five Little Dreidels

Have your children pretend to be dreidels. Recite the following rhyme and have them act out the movements as they hear them described.

Five little dreidels spinning in a row.

The first one spun, oh, so slow.

The second one went round and round.

The third one fell down on the ground.

The fourth one spun like a happy top.

The fifth one said, "I'll never stop!"

Five little dreidels, look and see,

Spinning at Hanukkah for you and me.

Marjorie Debowy

Latke Toppings

Set out a variety of toppings that are served with latkes, such as applesauce, sour cream, and yogurt. Let your children smell each of the toppings. Can they identify the toppings by scent alone? After you have made the Cheese Latkes on this page, let your children choose which toppings they would like on their latkes.

Cheese Latkes

Make these tasty Hanukkah latkes to share with everyone.

   3 eggs

¼ cup milk

   1 cup cottage cheese

¼ tsp. salt

   1 cup all-purpose flour

Use a blender to combine the eggs, milk, cottage cheese, and salt. Add flour and blend again. Spoon the batter into a hot, greased frying pan to make 3-inch rounds. Fry on both sides until golden brown. Drain on paper towels. Serve warm with sour cream, yogurt, or applesauce.

Christmas

Sorting Game

Cut out—in small, medium, and large sizes—green tree shapes, red candy cane shapes, and gold star shapes. Let your children take turns sorting the shapes by size, by color, or by kind. Have them line up each kind of shape in order, from smallest to largest.

Touching

Decorate the Tree

Set up a small real or artifical Christmas tree in your room. Have a box of nonbreakable Christmas ornaments near the tree. Let your children decorate and redecorate the tree as they wish. Talk about how the tree feels. Is it soft? Is it prickly? What do the ornaments feel like? At the end of the day, remove the ornaments from the tree and let the children start over again the next day.

...ell

...riety of bells, such as jingle ...gh bells, dinner bells, cow ...nd bird cage bells. Let your ...ren play the bells and listen to ...eir different sounds. Help them decide on a name for each of the bells. Out of sight of the children, play one of the bells. Have them listen carefully and tell you which bell they heard. Repeat with all the bells.

Smelling

Smells Like Christmas

Set aside a space on a table for collecting a variety of scented Christmas items. Bring in items as you find them, and encourage your children to do so as well. For example, you may want to include a pine cone, a candy cane, a peppermint scented candle, and a cinnamon stick. Let the children smell the various items as time allows.

Tasting

Easy Christmas Cookies

Purchase ready-made sugar cookie dough from your grocery store's refrigerator section. Let your children help you roll out the dough and use Christmas cookie cutters to cut out festive shapes. Have a jar of red and green sugar sprinkles available. Let the children shake some of the sprinkles on their cookies before baking them. Bake the cookies according to the package directions. Allow the cookies to cool slightly before eating them.

Kwanzaa

Seeing

Kwanzaa Placemats

Let your children try this version of African cloth dyeing to make placemats for snacktime. Have them dribble rubber cement in designs on sheets of white construction paper. Allow the glue to dry for about a half-hour. Then have the children brush red or green paint over the glue. When the paint is dry, let the children peel off the rubber cement to reveal the designs they have created.

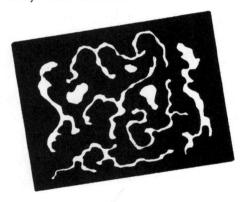

Touching

Kwanzaa Necklaces

For each of your children, cut a 24-inch length of yarn. Tie a bead to one end of the yarn and dip the other end in glue to make a "needle." Allow the glue to dry. Set out bowls of red, green, and black beads. Let your children string the beads on the yarn. When they are finished, cut off the stiff end of the yarn and tie the ends together. Let the children wear their Kwanzaa Necklaces during your Kwanzaa celebration.

Candle Rhyme

Cut out seven candle shapes, three from red paper, three from green paper, and one from black paper. Pass out the candle shapes to your children. Recite the rhyme below. Have the children listen carefully for their candle color. When they hear it, have them hold up their candles.

Red candles, green candles,

Black candle, too.

Will you light the candles?

Please, please do.

Red candles, green candles,

Black candle, too—

All shine at Kwanzaa

For me and you.

Gayle Bittinger

What Fruit Is It?

Cut up several fragrant, familiar fruits, such as a banana, an orange, and a watermelon. Put each fruit into a separate bowl. Invite one of your children to sit with you at a table. Have the child close his or her eyes. Hold up one of the bowls and let the child sniff. What fruit is it? Repeat with the other fruits.

Fruit Salad

Ask each of your children to bring in a fruit. Together, prepare the fruit for a salad. Gently mix the fruit together. Have the children set the table with their placemats from the Kwanzaa Placemats activity on the opposite page. Place the bowl of fruit salad on the table, along with a small bowl for each child. Let the children serve themselves.

Bread

What's Inside?

Purchase several different loaves of bread, such as white, whole-wheat, nut, and raisin swirl, from your local bakery. Ask that the bread not be sliced. Show the loaves to your children. Ask them if they can tell what the inside of the bread is like just by looking at the outside. Slice each loaf in half. How do the insides look the same? How do they look different?

Touching

Easy Breadsticks

Defrost frozen bread dough for two to three hours, or until the dough can be kneaded. Have your children sit around a clean table. Give each child a small piece of the dough. Show the children how to roll the dough between their hands to form a breadstick. Place the breadsticks on a greased baking sheet. Mix 1 egg white with 1 tablespoon water and brush it on the breadsticks. Sprinkle on poppy seeds or sesame seeds. Bake at 350°F for 15 to 20 minutes, or until browned.

Up! Comes the Bread!

Sing the following song with your children. Have them act out the motions of baking bread, as indicated in the song.

Sung to: "Pop! Goes the Weasel"

Mix the dough,

And add in the yeast.

Knead the bread so firmly.

Wait for awhile—

You'll have reason to smile.

Up! Comes the bread!

Diane Thom

Freshly Baked Bread

As you bake the breadsticks in the Easy Breadsticks activity on the opposite page, encourage your children to smell the bread baking. If the breadsticks are baking in another room, take your children there to smell them. If the breadsticks are baking close by, try taking the children outside for a bit and then coming back inside. Mmm!

Bread Smorgasbord

Serve a variety of breads for snack. Cut the loaves from the What's Inside? activity on the opposite page into slices. Spread butter or margarine on the bread slices and cut them into quarters. Let your children sample as many kinds of breads as they wish.

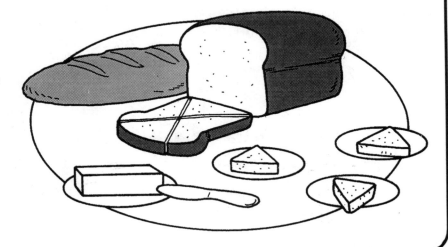

Peanut Butter

Seeing

Peanut Butter Dough

Make a simple picture recipe for making Peanut Butter Dough, as shown in the illustration. Help your children "read" the recipe. Let each child have a chance to make the dough after making sure hands are clean. Encourage the children to form the dough into various shapes before eating it.

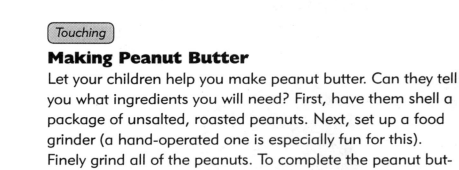

Touching

Making Peanut Butter

Let your children help you make peanut butter. Can they tell you what ingredients you will need? First, have them shell a package of unsalted, roasted peanuts. Next, set up a food grinder (a hand-operated one is especially fun for this). Finely grind all of the peanuts. To complete the peanut butter, mix the ground nuts with ¼ cup softened butter, and add salt to taste. Serve with apple slices, celery sticks, crackers, or toast.

Peanut Butter Rhyme

Teach your children the following rhyme. Let them act out the motions of making peanut butter as they are described.

Peanut butter, peanut butter, fun to chew.

Peanut butter, peanut butter, good for you.

First you take the peanuts and remove their shells.

Then you grind them up very well.

Peanut butter, peanut butter, now it's done.

Making peanut butter was lots of fun.

Peanut butter, peanut butter, fun to chew.

Peanut butter, peanut butter, good for you.

Susan Peters

Smelling

Comparing Scents

Set out three bowls: one with a few peanuts in their shells, another with a few shelled peanuts, and another filled with peanut butter. Let your children take turns sniffing the contents of each bowl. Do they smell exactly the same? Which one smells best? If they close their eyes, can they tell which one is which just by smelling?

Tasting

Creamy or Crunchy

Give each of your children a plate that has a small spoonful of creamy peanut butter, a small spoonful of crunchy peanut butter, and several soda crackers on it. Let your children use sturdy plastic knives or clean craft sticks to spread the peanut butter on their crackers. Let them taste the creamy and crunchy peanut butters. Do they taste the same? Which one do they like the best?

Apples

Seeing

Apple Sort

Collect three or four apples of several different varieties. Show your children the apples. Let them help you sort them by kind, color, or size. Can they think of any other ways to sort them? Which apple do they think looks the tastiest?

Touching

Exploring Apples

On a tray, arrange a variety of apples and parts of apples, such as seeds, a core, a few peelings, a stem, and an apple half. Let your children explore and touch all the different parts. Help them describe the way each part feels.

Hearing

The Apple Tree

Have your children stand in a circle around a pretend apple tree while you sing and act out the following song. You may wish to find a real apple tree with apples you can pick to circle around.

Sung to: "The Mulberry Bush"

Here we go round the apple tree,

Apple tree, apple tree.

Here we go round the apple tree

On a bright fall morning.

Let's all reach up and pick an apple,

Pick an apple, pick an apple.

Let's all reach up and pick an apple

On a bright fall morning.

Sue Schliecker

Smells So Good

Select three different kinds of apples
for this activity, such as a Red Delicious, a Granny Smith, and a Fuji.
Slice the apples and place each
apple's slices on a separate plate.
Let your children smell the different
apple slices. How do they smell alike?
How do they smell different?

Tasting

Apple Crisp

Make this simple apple crisp with your children. If you wish,
serve the warm crisp with slices of fresh apple. Let the children compare the taste of the two foods.

   4 baking apples

2/3 cup brown sugar

1/2 cup all-purpose flour

1/2 cup oats

3/4 tsp. cinnamon

3/4 tsp. nutmeg

1/3 cup margarine

Peel, core, and slice the apples. Place the apples in a
greased 8-inch-square baking pan. Mix the remaining ingredients together and sprinkle over the apples. Bake at
375°F for 30 minutes.

Bananas

Seeing

What's a Banana?

Show your children a small bunch of bananas. Have them notice how the bananas are attached at the stems. Ask the children to name all the colors they see. Remove one banana from the bunch and peel it. What color is the banana on the inside? If you wish, use the banana with the Mash This activity on this page, or break off small pieces for your children to eat.

Touching

Mash This

Let your children help you peel several bananas. Have them break each banana into several pieces and put the pieces into a resealable plastic bag. Squeeze the air out of the bags and seal them. Let the children use their hands and fingers to mash the banana pieces. Use the mashed bananas in the Banana Milkshake recipe on the opposite page or in your favorite banana recipe, such as banana bread.

Soft and Sweet

Sing the following song with your children.

Sung to: "Twinkle, Twinkle, Little Star"

Banana, banana, soft and sweet,

Banana, banana, good to eat.

Yummy on cereal, tasty alone,

Buy a bunch and take them home.

Banana, banana, soft and sweet,

Banana, banana, good to eat.

Beverly Qualheim

Smelling

Where's the Banana?

Peel and slice a banana and put it into a bowl. Have one of your children join you at a table. Ask the child to close his or her eyes. Place the bowl of banana slices on the table close to the child. Let the child use only the sense of smell to find the exact location of the bananas.

Tasting

Banana Milkshake

Place 2 ripe, mashed bananas, 1 cup milk, 1 cup orange juice, and 4 ice cubes in a blender. Whirl until smooth. Makes 8 small servings.

Strawberries

Strawberries Growing

Make a set of sequence cards, showing the various stages of a strawberry plant's growth. Let your children arrange the cards in order. If possible, let your children observe a real strawberry plant.

Touching

Picking Strawberries

Let your children help you prepare strawberries for a snack. Involve them in as many of the following steps as you can: picking strawberries, washing strawberries, hulling strawberries, slicing strawberries, and serving the strawberries.

Hearing

Summertime Treat

Say the following rhyme with your children.

Ten little strawberries on a vine.

I picked them, and they were mine.

I ate them all—they were so sweet.

They were the best summertime treat!

Gayle Bittinger

Scented Art

Cut large strawberry shapes out of
heavy paper. Mix strawberry gelatin
powder with water until the texture is
like paste. Let your children brush the
paste mixture over the strawberry
shapes. The paper strawberries will
smell like real ones, even after the
paste has dried.

Tasting

Dipping Strawberries

Serve your children plain strawberries
to taste and enjoy. Then set out one
or two dipping sauces for them to
sample. For example, let the children
dip their strawberries in vanilla yogurt
and toasted wheat germ, sour cream
and brown sugar, or, a sure favorite,
melted chocolate. Have your children
compare the tastes of the plain strawberries and the dipped strawberries.
Which one do they like the best?

Oranges

Seeing

Where's the Orange?

Hide an orange for each of your children around the room. Let the children look all over to find their oranges. Have them keep their oranges for the Orange Peeling activity on this page.

Touching

Orange Peeling

Encourage your children to feel the oranges they found in the Where's the Orange? activity on this page. What shape are the oranges? Does the skin feel bumpy or smooth? Help the children peel their oranges. Does the inside of the orange feel different from the outside? Show them how to pull their oranges into segments. If you wish, serve the orange segments at snacktime, or let the children eat them right away.

Hearing

Picking Oranges

Sing the following song to your children. Have them listen carefully and act out the motions as you sing about them.

Sung to: "Skip to My Lou"

Picking oranges from a tree,

Picking carefully, you see.

Picking oranges from a tree,

One for you and one for me.

Gayle Bittinger

Smelling

Orange Scents

Collect a variety of orange-flavored foods for your children to smell and compare. For example, you could set out orange juice, orange candy, orange drink mix, and orange flavoring. Also set out a real orange, cut in half. Let the children compare the scent of the real orange with those of the orange-flavored foods.

Tasting

Orange Juice

Let your children help you prepare freshly squeezed orange juice. Slice oranges in half. Let the children take turns holding their oranges over a pitcher, squeezing them, and watching the juice come out. You may wish to use a hand juicer to get all the remaining juice out of the orange halves. Strain out the seeds before serving the juice.

Watermelon

Seeing

Watermelon Art

Show your children a whole watermelon, the kind with seeds inside. Cut open the watermelon. What do your children see? Cut the watermelon into small pieces and remove the seeds. Set the seeds out to dry. Use the seedless watermelon pieces in the Juicy Treat activity on the opposite page. Give each of your children half a paper plate. Have the children color the rims of their plates green and the centers pink or red, then let the children glue the real watermelon seeds to their plates.

Touching

Checking It Out

Give your children a whole watermelon to examine. Let them measure the melon with a measuring tape. Can they lift the melon? Encourage the children to predict what might happen if they put the melon into water. Would it sink or float? Let them test their predictions in a sink or a bathtub.

Watermelon Seed Shaker

Let your children help you collect the seeds from a watermelon. Set the seeds out to dry. Give each child two plain paper cups and several of the watermelon seeds. Have the children put the seeds in one of their cups and place the other cup on top, rim to rim. Tape each child's cups together. Let the children use red, black, and green paint to paint their cups to look like watermelons. Allow the paint to dry completely. Have the children use their watermelon shakers as they listen to music. Encourage them to shake along to the beat.

Juicy Treat

For each of your children, put several watermelon chunks into a resealable plastic bag. Show the children how to gently squish the watermelon chunk into juice. Help each child put a plastic drinking straw into one corner of his or her bag. Let the children enjoy drinking their tasty watermelon juice.

Smells So Sweet

Let your children smell a whole watermelon. What does it smell like? Does it smell good to eat? Now cut open the watermelon. Give each child a slice of it. Have them smell their watermelon slices. What do they smell like? Let them enjoy scent of their watermelon while they eat it.

Carrots

Seeing

Carrots and Tops

Give each of your children a carrot with the green top attached. Tell your children that you will say a word that describes either the orange or the green part of their carrots. Ask them to point to the part of the carrot you are describing. For example, if you say, "leafy," they would point to the top. If you say, "smooth," they would point to the actual carrot. Continue with as many descriptive words as possible.

Touching

Fixing Carrots

If possible, take your children to a garden where they can pick their own carrots to eat. After they have their carrots (either from a garden or store-bought), show them how to prepare them for eating. Have them break off the tops of their carrots, scrub them under water, and, if you wish, peel them. Slice the carrots into sticks and let the children enjoy them at snack time.

Is It a Carrot?

Have your children sit in front of you. Turn around so they cannot see your face. Ask them to listen while you take a bite of bread or carrot. Turn around. Can they tell which one you are chewing? Try it again. Then give each child a small piece of bread and a carrot stick. Have them listen for the difference in the way the carrot and bread sound when they are chewed. This may also be a good time to talk about chewing as quietly as possible, even when you are chewing something noisy like carrots.

Smelling

Grating Carrots

Let your children help you scrub and peel some carrots. Help them grate the carrots. What do the children smell? How do carrots smell? Do they smell salty, sour, or sweet? Use the grated carrots in the Carrot Gelatin Salad recipe on this page.

Tasting

Carrot Gelatin Salad

With your children, prepare a package of orange gelatin according to the directions. Before placing the gelatin in the refrigerator to set, let the children stir in one or two grated carrots. Allow the gelatin to set, then serve. How do carrots taste when served this way? Let the children compare the taste of the carrots in the gelatin with carrot sticks. Which one do they like the best?

Corn

Colorful Corn

Set out several ears of colorful Indian corn for your children to examine. What colors do they see? Remove the kernels from the Indian corn. Let the children use the colorful kernels to create collages on heavy paper.

Shucking Corn

Cover a table with newspaper and set out a bucket or a bowl of corn to be shucked. Show your children how to remove the husk and silk from each ear of corn. Let them work at shucking the corn. Place a big pan in the center of the table to hold the shucked corn. Use the corn in the Yummy Corn activity on the opposite page.

Popcorn Popping

Out of sight of your children, begin
popping some popcorn. When they
begin to hear the popping sound, ask
them if they know what it is. When
they guess that it's popcorn popping,
ask them to keep on listening and tell
you when it's all done. Then let everyone enjoy a handful or two of the
freshly popped corn, or use it with the
Scented Toppings activity on this page.

Smelling

Scented Toppings

Set out a variety of different popcorn
toppings in separate bowls. For example, you could provide melted butter, salt, garlic salt, Parmesan cheese,
and cinnamon sugar. Let your children
smell the topping in each bowl. Do
any of the toppings smell sweet? What
about salty? Let each child select a
topping to put on some popcorn.

Tasting

Yummy Corn

Use the shucked ears of corn from the
Shucking Corn activity on the opposite
page. Boil the corn in a pan of water
for 3 to 5 minutes, or until done. Allow
the corn to cool slightly. Serve the corn
to your children.

Potatoes

Seeing

Potato Comparison

Collect a variety of different kinds of potatoes, such as baking, russet, Yukon gold, and red. Let your children examine the potatoes. How are they alike? How are they different? Set out a basket. Let the children take turns arranging the potatoes in the basket to display on a table.

Touching

Digging for Potatoes

Fill a large bucket or barrel with dirt. Bury 10 to 20 potatoes in the dirt. Talk with your children about how potatoes grow in the dirt. Ask them to think about how a farmer might harvest potatoes. Then show them the bucket of dirt. Let the children gently dig through the dirt and "harvest" the potatoes in it.

Hearing

Five Little Potatoes

Say the following rhyme with your children. Have them listen carefully and act out the motions, as indicated.

Five little potatoes were growing in the ground,
(Hold up five fingers.)

Covered up with rich soil, making not a sound.
(Place other hand over fingers.)

Down came the rain one stormy summer day.
(Flutter fingers downward.)

The five little potatoes slept the day away.
(Rest cheek on folded hands.)

Out came the sun—the farmer came out, too.
(Walk in place.)

She dug up those potatoes to give to me and you.
(Pretend to dig.)

Mildred Hoffman

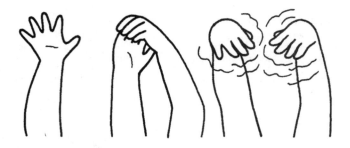

Smells Great

Let your children help you scrub some potatoes. Cut each potato into eight wedges. Set aside one or two potato wedges. Place the remaining wedges on a baking sheet and, if desired, sprinkle them with salt. Bake them at 500°F for 15 to 20 minutes. When they are done, place them on a plate. Let the children compare the scent of the uncooked potato wedges with the cooked ones. Which one smells best? Use the oven-baked potatoes with the Comparing Tastes activity on this page.

Tasting

Comparing Tastes

Let your children help you make mashed potatoes. Then make a simple bar graph as shown in the illustration. Give each of your children a potato cutout with his or her name on it. Set out the mashed potatoes and the oven-baked potatoes from the Smells Great activity on this page. Let the children sample a little of each kind. Have the children place their potato cutouts on the graph under the potato they liked the best.

We Like These Potatoes

Teran   Kelsey
Jennifer Phillip
Alisha   Keesha
Meggan   Alex
Rory
Matt

Eggs

What's Inside?

Collect as many different sizes and colors of chicken eggs as you can. (A local farm may be able to supply you with eggs of varying shades of brown, green, and blue.) Show your children the eggs. How do the eggs look alike? How do they look different? Can the children tell what is inside the eggs by looking at the outside? Crack open each egg into its own bowl. Let the children compare the insides of the eggs. Do the insides all look the same? Combine all the eggs into one bowl and use with the Cooking Smells activity on the opposite page.

Touching

Peeling Eggs

Give each of your children a plate with a hard-cooked egg on it. Let your children peel their eggs. What do the shells feel like? What do the insides of the eggs feel like? Use the peeled eggs with the Deviled Eggs activity on the opposite page.

Scrambled Eggs

Read the following rhyme to your children.

I like my eggs up.

I like my eggs down.

I like my eggs scrambled

And scrambled around.

I like my eggs scrambled

With hot, buttered toast.

I like my eggs scrambled,

Yes, scrambled the most!

Lois E. Putnam

Tasting

Deviled Eggs

Use the peeled, hard-cooked eggs from the Peeling Eggs activity on the opposite page. Cut each egg in half lengthwise. Take out the yolks and place them in a bowl. Stir in a small amount of mayonnaise and mustard. Add salt and pepper to taste. Give each of your children a plate with two egg white halves and a small scoop of the yolk mixture on it. Let your children taste a little of the egg white and a little of the yolk mixture. Then let them use spoons to scoop the yolk mixture into their egg whites to make Deviled Eggs.

Smelling

Cooking Smells

Take the cracked eggs from the What's Inside? activity on the opposite page. Have your children smell the eggs. Add 1 tablespoon of water for each egg in the bowl. Let the children take turns whipping the eggs and water together. How do the eggs smell now? Scramble the eggs. Encourage the children to smell the eggs as they cook and eat them.

Pie

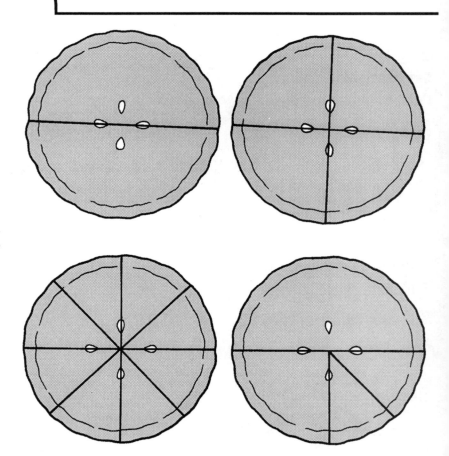

Pie Slices

Cut three pie shapes out of tan construction paper. Decorate the tops to look like pie crust, if you wish. Cut one pie shape into halves, one into quarters, and one into eighths. Show your children the pies. Let them take turns putting the pie slices together to make whole pies. Challenge older children to make a pie using at least one slice from each of the original pies.

Making a Pie

Let your children help you make a pie. Purchase ready-made pie dough (enough for two crusts) from your grocery store's refrigerator section, or make the dough yourself. Let the children roll out half the dough. This will be the bottom crust. Place the crust in a pie pan and add the desired filling. Have the children roll out the remaining dough for the top crust. Let each child pierce the crust once with a fork. Bake the pie according to the recipe or package directions. When the pie is cool, serve each child a small slice. Talk about how they used their hands to help make it.

Hearing

Pie Game

Give each of your children a pie pan or a pie shape cut out of heavy paper. Have each child sit in front of an "oven," such as a chair, a box, a shelf, or a table. Give the children directions about what to do with their "pies," for example, "Put your pie in the oven. Take your pie out of the oven. Trade pies with someone else." Continue as long as interest lasts.

Smelling

Pie Scents

Give your children paper plates. Have the children decorate their plates with brown crayons to make them look like pies. When they are finished, let them brush glue over their crayon designs and sprinkle on ground cinnamon or apple pie spice. Encourage them to smell the wonderful "pies" they have just made.

Tasting

Biscuit Pies

Let your children make these simple pies with their favorite jam or jelly. Give each child one refrigerator biscuit. Show the children how to flatten the biscuits with their hands. Offer two or three choices of jam or jelly and put one small spoonful in the middle of each child's biscuit. Help the children fold their biscuits in half and place them on a baking sheet. Use a toothpick to write each child's name on a small strip of foil and put it under his or her biscuit. Bake the biscuits according to the package directions. Allow the pies to cool before serving them.

Zoo

Zoo List

Before going to the zoo with your children, discuss the animals and other points of interest you might see there. Make a picture list of those items, with a box in front of each one. Take your list to the zoo. Occasionally remind the children of the things on the list. Have them be on the lookout for those items. Check off each item as it is seen.

Touching

Touch the Animals

As you and your children look at each animal, imagine what it would feel like. Does the animal's fur or skin look rough or smooth, soft or hard? Visit the Children's Zoo or Petting Zoo. Let the children gently touch and pet the animals there, as permitted.

Zoo Sounds

Each time you see an animal, stop and listen. Is it making a sound? Can you hear it talking? Can you hear it breathing or snorting? Afterwards, talk about the loud and quiet animals you heard.

Smelling

Zoo Smells

As you walk around the zoo, alert your children to the variety of smells, such as the smell of animals, flowers, trees, and even popcorn from the food vendors. At the end of your visit, ask the children which smells they liked best. Have them imagine they are one of the animals. Which smell would they like now?

Tasting

Animal Foods

Let your children taste some of the foods that the animals they see at the zoo like to eat, such as bananas, peanuts, carrots, apples, and nuts. Encourage them to tell you which animals would like to eat which foods.

Farm

Seeing

Mothers and Babies

When you arrive at the farm, have your children be sure to look for mother animals with their babies. Each time they see a pair, write down the name of the animal. At the end of the day, count how many mamas and how many babies were seen.

Touching

Petting the Animals

Make arrangements ahead of time with the farm to allow your children to pet some of the animals. Talk about how to act around the animals, about moving slowly, using whisper voices, and being very gentle. Let the children pet the animals. Help them describe the way each animal's fur or feathers feels.

Listening Game

Take a tape recorder with you to the farm. While you are there, record the different animals "talking." Replay the tape when you are back in your room. Have your children listen carefully to identify all the animal sounds they hear.

Smelling

Farm Smells

When you are at the farm, ask your children to take a good sniff. Why do they think a farm smells the way it does? Ask them to look around and name some of the things they are smelling: manure, hay, animals, feed, and so on.

Tasting

Farm Snack

Talk with your children about some of the foods that are produced on a farm, such as eggs, milk, vegetables, and fruits. Prepare a variety of these foods for your children to sample at snacktime.

Beach

Beach Views

When your children are at the beach, have them look around carefully. What is the beach made of it? Is it sandy or rocky? Do they see any plants? Shells? Animals? Are there a lot of people? Is the water rough or smooth? Encourage them to describe everything they see.

Touching

Beach Game

Challenge your children with this touching game. Ask each of them to find something that feels smooth. After they have shown it to you, have them put it back where they found it. Continue with other descriptive words, such as rough, soft, hard, cold, and warm.

Splash!

Have your children throw rocks into the water. (Be sure to establish a few safety rules ahead of time; for example, rocks may be thrown only from a certain point toward the water.) Ask your children to listen carefully to the splash each rock makes. Do different rocks make different sounds? What type of rock makes the quietest sound? What rock makes the loudest sound?

Smelling

Fresh Sea Air

When you first arrive at the beach, have your children take a moment to smell their surroundings. What do they smell? Can they smell the fresh air? The seawater? Blossoming flowers? Wet sand? Encourage them to keep their noses ready to sniff any new scents that come their way.

Tasting

Sandy Beach Picnic

Ahead of time, prepare an easy snack or lunch and place it in a picnic basket. Have your children help you spread blankets out on the beach to sit on while they eat. Serve the children from the basket.

Forest

Seeing

Forest Book

When your children visit the forest, bring along your camera. Take photographs of all the interesting sights and places the children find. Put the developed photos in a book for the children to look at. Ask them to tell you what they see in each photo, remembering when they were there and saw it themselves.

Touching

Explore a Tree

Let your children choose a tree to explore with their hands. Ask them to find out what the tree's bark, roots, branches, leaves, and so on, feel like. Which part is the smoothest? Which is the roughest? If you wish, have the children describe how two different trees feel.

Forest Sounds

Have your children sit or stand in place and be very, very still. Ask them to close their eyes and just listen. What do they hear? If necessary, help the children hear the sounds by pointing them out as you hear them. Can they identify every sound they hear?

Smelling

Forest Smells

Have your children smell the forest. What do they smell? Can they smell the trees, dirt, flowers, bushes, or ripening berries? Which smell do they like the best? Do different parts of the forest smell different?

Tasting

Forest Snack

Take along a snack to eat in the forest. While your children are eating, talk about the berries and nuts that grow in the forest. Caution the children to never eat forest plants without asking a grownup first because, while some are safe to eat, others are poisonous and would make them sick. After everyone is finished eating their snack, be sure any litter is picked up.

Flowers

Forsythia Flowers

Cut vase shapes out of colorful patterned paper, such as wallpaper samples or wrapping paper. Let each of your children select one of the vase shapes and glue it to a sheet of construction paper. Have the children draw several stems coming out of their vases with brown crayons or felt tip markers. Then show them how to paint little yellow X's along their stems to make forsythia blossoms. When the children are finished, set out a vase of real forsythia. Let the children compare their works of art to the flowers in the vase. How are they alike? How are they different? (Be sure the children understand that their pictures are not supposed to look exactly like the real flowers.)

Touching

Explore a Rose

Provide several roses for your children to explore. (A florist shop may donate roses that would otherwise have to be discarded.) Let them discover the soft, sharp, rough, and smooth parts of the flower. Have the children close their eyes and give them a petal and a leaf to touch. Can they tell which is which?

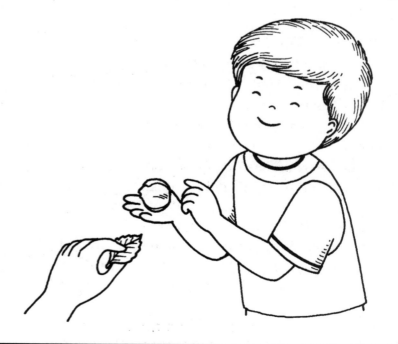

I'm Smelling Flowers

Give each of your children a real or pretend flower. Sing the following song and have the children act out the motions while they hold their flowers.

Sung to: "It's Raining, It's Pouring"

I'm smelling,

I'm smelling.

My nose is busy smelling.
(Hold flower to nose.)

First this way,
(Hold flower to one side.)

And then that way,
(Hold flower to other side.)

My nose is busy smelling.
(Hold flower to nose.)

Kathy McCullough

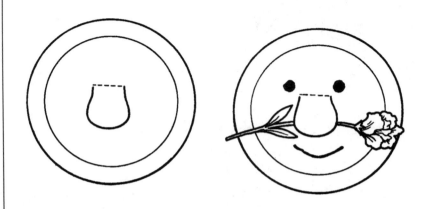

Smelling

This Flower Smells Best

Collect a variety of flowers for your children to smell. Which ones smell nice? Which ones do not? Give each child a paper plate that has been prepared, as shown in the illustration, by drawing and cutting along a rounded nose outline. Let the children add eyes and a mouth to their plates. Let each child select a flower to slip under the nose cutout. Tape the flower in place on the back of the plate.

Tasting

Flower Tasting Fun

Prepare a simple "flower" snack for each of your children by arranging apple slices or orange segments around a strawberry or a few grapes on a plate. Talk with the children about how bees fly from flower to flower, collecting the nectar to take home to their hives. Ask your children to pretend to be bees. Tell them that you have prepared a special flower snack for them to fly to and eat. One at a time, have the "bees" fly to the "flowers" and enjoy their snack.

Rain

Seeing

I See the Rain

Watch the rain with your children. Is it raining a little or a lot? Have the children put on rain clothes and go outside. Can they see the raindrops falling on the ground? On the trees? In puddles? Where does the rain go? Have them follow a stream of rain to a puddle or a storm drain. Continue with the activity below.

Touching

Raindrops on My Face

While your children are still outside, let them feel the rain as it falls on their hands and faces. Does the rain feel warm or cold? Are the drops soft or hard?

Variation: Let your children feel the "rain" indoors. Poke a few holes in the bottom of an old plastic container. Hold the container over a sink, fill it with water, and shake it gently back and forth. Have the children take turns putting their hands under the container to feel the "rain."

Rainstorm

Have your children sit in a circle. Say the following rhyme.
Have your children act out the motions, as indicated.

I hear thunder, I hear rain.
(Cup hand behind ear.)

Can you help me make the same?

Raindrops falling, falling down.

Can you help me make their sound?
(Slap hands on floor.)

Softly first the raindrops fall.
(Slap hands softly.)

Now make your fingers form a ball.
(Make fists and pound them on floor.)

Faster, faster, the raindrops come—
(Pound fists faster.)

Sounds like pounding on a drum.

What a racket, what a sound.

I wish this storm would please calm down.
(Make pounding quieter and quieter, then stop.)

Now the storm is gone at last.

I'm just glad this storm has passed.

Patty Claycomb

Smelling

After the Storm

After a big rainstorm has come and gone, take your children outside. Have them close their eyes, stand still, and just concentrate on smelling. Can they smell the fresh scent of rain? If possible, purchase an air freshener with the "fresh rain" scent. Let your children compare the real scent and the purchased scent. Which one do they like best?

Tasting

Rainy Day Snack

Set up several large umbrellas around the room. Let your children sit under the umbrellas while they eat their snack. If it is raining, be sure to arrange the umbrellas in places where they can watch the rain.

Rainbows

Finding Rainbows

While your children are occupied, put a small, rectangular mirror into a clear glass and fill the glass with water. Place the glass in a sunny window and position the mirror so that it catches the sunlight and creates a rainbow on a wall. Ask your children to find the rainbow in your room. When they find it, help them name the colors they see. Which color is on the top? Which one is on the bottom? Try positioning the mirror and glass in other ways to create rainbows in other parts of your room.

Touching

Rainbow Mural

Cut a rainbow shape out of a large piece of heavy paper. Cut the shape into six arcs. Set out the largest arc. Have the children work together to cover the arc with the color red. Encourage them to color the arc with red crayons or felt tip markers, glue on red paper or fabric, or think of other ways to make it red. Repeat with each of the other arcs, from largest to smallest, in this order: orange, yellow, green, blue, purple. Hang the arcs, one under the other, to create a colorful rainbow.

Rainbow Game

Have your children stand around the room. Ask them to listen carefully as you say lots of different words about rainbows (red, orange, yellow, green, blue, purple, rain, sun, pretty, sky, etc.). Tell them that whenever they hear the word "rainbow," they should find a partner and make a rainbow arc with their arms. Continue as long as interest lasts.

Smelling

Rainbow Smells

Set out a bowl of red strawberries; orange slices; yellow lemon slices; green honeydew melon chunks; blue blueberries; and purple grapes, cut in half. Let your children take turns smelling this colorful rainbow of scents. Which one is their favorite?

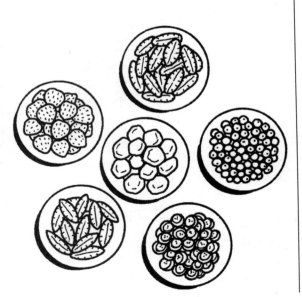

Tasting

Frozen Rainbow Treats

Prepare frozen orange juice concentrate, using only two cans of water instead of the usual three. Repeat for cranapple juice concentrate and grape juice concentrate. Place 24 small cups on a baking sheet. Fill each cup not quite 1/3 full with the cranapple juice. Place a clean craft stick in each cup. Allow to freeze for several hours, until nearly solid. Add the same amount of orange juice to each cup and freeze again. Repeat with the grape juice. Freeze the treats overnight before serving. Let your children enjoy the taste of the rainbow treats.

Mud

Seeing

A Recipe for Mud

Make a picture recipe for your children to follow to make their own mud out of dirt and water. (See illustration. Your recipe may vary depending on the dirt you use.) Set out a pan of dirt, a small pitcher of water, and some small measuring cups. Encourage your children to look at the chart and follow the directions.

Touching

Squish Between the Toes

Prepare a dishpan of mud. Set the pan on some newspaper or an old vinyl tablecloth. Let your children take turns taking off their shoes and socks, sitting on a low chair, and putting their feet in the mud. How does it feel? Does it squish between their toes? Is it cold? Have a tub of warm, soapy water available to wash their feet afterwards.

Mud Everywhere

Recite the following rhyme with your children. Have them act out the motions as they listen to the rhyme.

Mud on my fingers,
(Hold up fingers.)

Mud on my toes,
(Touch toes.)

Mud in my hair,
(Point to hair.)

And mud on my nose!
(Touch nose.)

Mud squishing here,
(Cup hand above eye and look to the left.)

Mud squishing there,
(Cup hand above eye and look to the right.)

Mud squishing all around,
(Look all around.)

And everywhere!
(Hold up hands.)

Gayle Bittinger

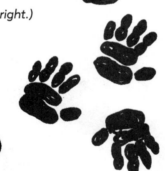

Mud Pie

Explain to your children that there is a real dessert called Mud Pie. It is not made with mud. Let them help you make this simplified version of Mud Pie. Give each child a clear plastic cup and two chocolate cookies. Have them each crumble one of their cookies and place the crumbs in their cups. Prepare instant chocolate pudding. Let each child place a scoop of the pudding in his or her cup. Have the children crumble their remaining cookies and sprinkle the crumbs on the pudding. Ask the children if they can think of any reasons why this dessert would be called Mud Pie. (It looks like a pie made from mud, it has the texture of mud, etc.) Be sure to emphasize the difference between this edible Mud Pie and a mud pie they might make outside. Let the children enjoy their edible Mud Pie desserts.

Muddy Nose

Encourage your children to smell the mud they made in the mud-making activity on the opposite page. What does it smell like? Does the smell remind them of anything? Do they like the smell?

Sand

Seeing

Observing Sand

Cover the bottom of a pan with dark construction paper and sprinkle some sand on top. Let your children take turns using a magnifying glass to look at the grains of sand. What do the grains look like? Are they all the same? Explain that sand is made up of rocks and shells that have been ground into tiny, tiny pieces. Set out some rocks and shells. Encourage the children to compare the whole rocks and shells with the tiny grains of sand.

Touching

Wet and Dry Sand

Set up two dishpans outside on the ground or inside on a low table. Fill one dishpan with dry sand. Fill the other dishpan with wet sand. Let your children take turns using their hands to feel the differences in the two kinds of sand. Which one do they like best?

Sand Shakers

Give each of your children a plastic container with a lid. (Clear plastic containers work especially well, because the children can see the sand as well as hear it.) Have the children fill their containers about halfway with sand. Help the children glue the lids to the containers. Allow the glue to dry. How does the sand sound? Is it loud or quiet? Let the children use their shakers to keep the beat of the music you play.

Smelling

Sandpaper Scents

Select a heavy-grit sandpaper (the roughest you can find). Cut the sheets of sandpaper into quarters. Show your children one of the quarter sheets of sandpaper. Let them feel the roughness. Explain to them that tiny grains of sand have been glued to the paper in a special way, to make it rough. Can they tell you some of the things that can be done with sandpaper? Tell them that the sandpaper can also be used to give off a wonderful scent. Give each child one of the sandpaper quarters and a whole cinnamon stick. Show the children how to rub the cinnamon stick across the sandpaper to slightly grate the cinnamon stick and release its fragrance.

Tasting

Follow the Footprints

Take your children to a sandy beach. Place their snack in a sealed container and hide it behind a bush or a log. Have the children follow your footprints to find their hidden snack. If a beach is not nearby, hide the snack outside and have your children follow paper footprints to find it.

Rocks

Seeing

Rock Collections

Arrange an assortment of rocks on a table. Let the children look at them. Can they think of ways to sort them? By color? By size? By most and least favorite? Set out a baking pan, a cup of water, and an eye dropper. Let the children take turns placing a rock in the pan and using the eye dropper to cover it with water. Does the rock look different when it is wet?

Touching

More Rock Collections

Take your children on a walk outside to collect rocks. Encourage them to especially look for rocks with interesting textures. Can they find a smooth rock? A rough rock? A bumpy rock? Help the children describe the various textured rocks they find.

Hearing

Rock Music

Place an assortment of rocks in the middle of the floor and invite your children to sit around them. Select two of the rocks and have the children listen as you tap them together. Select two different rocks and tap them together. Were the sounds the same or different? Continue, with your children's help, tapping together a variety of rocks. Let them explore how size, shape, and kind of rock affect the sounds the rocks make.

Grinding Rocks

Let your children help you find a large, flat rock and a smaller rock they can hold in one hand. Clean and scrub the rocks very well. Set out a variety of whole spices and grains, such as cinnamon sticks, mustard seeds, peppercorns, wheat berries, and oats. Show the children how to use the rocks to grind the spices and grains. Have them smell each spice or grain before and after the grinding. Explain that this is a very old way humans have used—and still use, in some places—to grind foods to eat.

Tasting

Stone Soup

Tell the story "Stone Soup" to your children. (Your library should have a copy of this old folktale.) What kind of stone or rock do they think was used to make the soup? Let the children help you select a rock to use in making their own Stone Soup. First, thoroughly clean the rock. Place the rock in a pan and add water and bouillon cubes. Bring the water to a boil. Let the children help you add other soup ingredients that you have prepared. If you wish, retell the story as you make the soup. Let the soup simmer for a while, then allow it to cool before serving.

Bubbles

Super Bubbles

Make giant bubble wands by bending coat hangers into a variety of shapes, as shown in the illustration. Pour a 1-inch layer of bubble mixture into a shallow pan. Let your children take turns using the bubble wands to make beautiful, giant bubbles. Encourage them to move the wands through the air slowly to make the largest bubbles. How far up can they see their bubbles float?

Touching

Popping Bubbles

In a large indoor room, or outside, blow lots of bubbles. Let your children pop all the bubbles they can. Now, tell your children that you want them to pop the bubbles, but this time they can only use their elbows. Blow more bubbles. Repeat with other body parts, as desired.

Bubble Game

Have your children pretend to be bubbles. Ask them to float carefully all around the room. Softly repeat the phrase, "Float, float, little bubbles," then suddenly say "Pop!" When the children hear the word "pop," have them pretend that their bubbles have burst, and they are falling to the ground. Continue as long as interest lasts.

Tasting

Tiny Bubbles

Serve your children sparkling apple cider in clear plastic cups. Have them notice all the bubbles. Can they feel the bubbles on their tongue when they drink their juice?

Hint: Instead of buying sparkling apple cider, make your own by combining, in a pitcher, 1 (12-oz.) can frozen apple juice concentrate, 3 cups water, and 1 (1-liter) bottle club soda.

Smelling

Scented Bubbles

Add some scented bubble bath to your water table or to a sink or a pan of water. Let your children play with the bubbles while they enjoy the scent. If you wish, vary the scent from day to day. Each day, ask the children if they can identify the new scent.

Water

Seeing

It's All the Same

Collect 1-cup containers in a variety of shapes (tall, short, wide, curvy, etc.). Set out the containers, a pitcher of water, and a 1-cup measuring cup. Ask your children to predict how much water the first container will hold, then pour in 1 cup of water. Ask them if they see any other container that will hold that same amount. Test their hypotheses. Let them discover that each container, even though it looks different, holds the same amount of water.

Touching

Water Table Fun

Let your children explore water in a water table, a dishpan of water, a sink filled with water, or a bucket of water outside. Put a variety of plastic containers in the water. Let them pour, measure, dump, and fill the containers with water.

Water Sounds

Tape record as many different water sounds as you can find; for example, the toilet flushing; water running into a sink, a bathtub, or a washing machine; a lawn sprinkler running; a squirt bottle squirting; and so on. Play the tape for your children. Let them listen carefully and try to identify the source of each sound.

Smelling

Flavored Waters

Purchase several of the flavored waters that are available. Pour a small amount of each kind of water into a separate glass. Put out the glasses and the bottles (with the lids on). Let your children take turns smelling the waters. Can they match the picture on the front of the bottle with the matching scent?

Tasting

Drinking Water

Prepare two small pitchers, one with ice-cold water and one with water at room temperature. Set out the pitchers and some cups. Let your children take turns pouring the two different waters and comparing their taste. Which one do they like best? If you wish, make a graph and let each child put an X by the water temperature he or she prefers to drink.

Leaves

Seeing

Leaf Prints

On a fall day, take your children outside after a rain. Have them notice how the wet leaves shine and stick to the ground like glue. One at a time, let them pick up a leaf and place it on a sheet of dark construction paper. Press firmly, then lift to see a leaf print. If you wish, help the children use a fine point marker to outline their leaf shapes before the water evaporates.

Touching

Leaf Pool

Set up a small, inflatable pool. Fill the pool with dry fall leaves. Let your children explore the leaves with their hands and bodies. What do the leaves feel like? Can they tell the size of a leaf just by touching it?

Hearing

Autumn Leaves

Sing the following song with your children. Have them act out the motions, as indicated.

Sung to: "Frère Jacques"

I'm a tree, I'm a tree.
   (Hold arms in air.)

Look at me, look at me.
   (Point to self.)

Autumn leaves are falling,
   (Shake fingers from above head to ground.)

Autumn leaves are falling

All around, all around.
   (Move hands on ground around self.)

Rosemary Giordano

Fragrant Leaves

Let your children compare the scents of a variety of leaves—dry, green, wet, crumpled, and so on. Include leaves from fragrant plants, such as sage, eucalyptus, and basil, too. How are they alike? How are they different? Do different kinds of leaves smell different? Have each child hold up or point to the leaf they like to smell the most.

Tasting

Leafy Snack

Explain to your children that trees are not the only plants that have leaves—lettuce and cabbage do, too. Let the children help you wash and gently dry the leaves from a head of lettuce. For each child, place a lettuce leaf on a plate and top with a scoop of gelatin, cottage cheese, tuna salad, or fruit cocktail.

Ice

Seeing

Ice Catchers

Do this activity when you know you'll have below-freezing temperatures for several days in a row. Give each of your children a metal pie pan. Let the children arrange evergreen sprigs, dried flowers, and wild berries in their pans. Arrange a length of yarn in each child's pan to be used as a hanger. Add water and take the pans outside to freeze. After the water has frozen, take the translucent Ice Catchers out of the pans and hang them around the yard.

Touching

Ice Cube Fun

Have each of your children bring in an ice cube tray from home. Set out several small pitchers or measuring cups full of water. Help the children add a different color of food coloring to each container and stir well. Let the children use eyedroppers to fill the compartments of their ice cube trays with the colored water of their choice. Freeze the ice cube trays for at least three hours, or overnight. When the ice cubes are frozen, give the children their trays and let them experiment with the ice cubes. Encourage them to stack or arrange the ice cubes on plates or trays. Let them add the ice cubes to a water table to see what happens. Have them put two different colors of ice cubes into a glass to see what new color the melting ice makes.

Hearing

Icy Counting

Have your children sit in a circle. Arrange a bowl of ice cubes and an empty bowl behind a screen so your children cannot see them. Have the children listen as you drop one of the ice cubes into the empty bowl. Ask them to listen carefully and count each time they hear that sound. Drop five ice cubes, one at a time, into the bowl. Count along with them. Ask them how many ice cubes they heard. Repeat several times with different numbers of ice cubes.

Smelling

Flavored Ice

Use a variety of juices to make ice cubes. Give each of your children one of each kind of ice cube. Let the children sniff the ice to identify the different flavors. When they have discovered all the flavors, have each child put his or her ice cubes in a glass. Fill the glasses with juice and let the children enjoy their own special juice drink.

Tasting

Fancy Ice

Set out several ice cubes trays and small chunks of fruit, such as grapes, cantaloupe, honeydew, blueberries, strawberries, and raspberries. Let your children take turns placing one or two pieces of fruit in each segment of the ice cube trays. Fill the trays with water. Allow the water to freeze. Let the children use their Fancy Ice to chill room-temperature juice.

Bears

Seeing

Bears and Teddy Bears

Collect a variety of teddy bears and some photographs of real bears. Show them to your children. Ask your children to look carefully at both kinds of bears. What are some ways they are alike? What are some ways they are different?

Touching

Hug a Bear

Talk about bear hugs with your children. Use a large teddy bear to demonstrate a bear hug. Let the children take turns giving the teddy bear a bear hug. Would they want to hug a real bear?

Hearing

Wake Up Bears!

Read the following rhyme to your children. Have them pretend to be the waking bears and act out all the motions as they are described.

Wake up bears, spring is here.

Jump out of bed, look everywhere.

See the sun, touch the trees,

Taste the honey, hear the bees.

Smell the flowers, each pretty daisy.

Use your senses, don't be lazy!

Margo Miller

Berry Scents

Set out bowls of various kinds of berries. Tell your children that bears love to eat berries. Let them sniff the berries in each bowl. If they were bears, which berries would they like the best? Let them have a sample of each berry, if you wish.

Tasting

Snacking on Honey

Set the table with plates of buttered toast and a jar of honey. Have your children pretend to be bears and lumber around the room in search of honey. When they "find" the honey on the table, have them sit down. Help each child drizzle a small amount of honey on their toast. Let the children enjoy their delicious honey treat. (*Note:* Children under the age of one should not eat honey.)

Cats

Where's the Mouse?

Explain to your children that cats can see very well. Have them pretend to be cats. Hide a toy mouse in the room. Have the "cats" look all around for the mouse. How quickly can they find it? Continue hiding the mouse as long as interest lasts.

Touching

Pet the Cat

Arrange for a real cat, one with a calm, tolerant personality, to visit your room. Talk with your children ahead of time about the way to pet an animal. Remind them that quiet voices and soft movements are best, so they won't scare the animal. When the cat arrives, let a few children at a time pet it. What does the cat's fur feel like? Is it rough or smooth?

Variation: Instead of having a cat visit your room, have several stuffed toy cats available. Let your children take turns petting these cats.

Cat Dance

Sing this version of the "Hokey-Pokey" to your children. Let them pretend to be cats and do the motions with you.

Sung to: "Hokey-Pokey"

You put your cat paws in,

You put your cat paws out,

You put your cat paws in,

And you shake them all about.

You do the Hokey-Pokey,

And you turn yourself around.

That's what it's all about!

Additional verses: You put your cat whiskers in; You put your cat ears in; You put your cat tail in.

Gayle Bittinger

Smelling

Sniff, Sniff

Prepare a variety of smelling cups. (See page 45 for directions for making smelling cups.) Have your children pretend to be cats while they sniff the cups. If they like what they are smelling, have them "purr." If they don't like what they are smelling, have them "meow."

Tasting

Bowl of Milk

Pretend your children are cats. Serve your "cats" bowls of milk as you call them by their cat names. Show your cats how to carefully lift their bowls up to drink from them. Let your cats thank you for their milk by purring loudly.

Dogs

A Dog Visit

Make arrangements for a calm, friendly dog to visit your room. Have your children sit quietly as they look at the dog. Point out the dog's tail, paws, legs, ears, nose, eyes, and so on. If you wish, invite one or two children at a time to come up and gently pet the dog.

Variation: Instead of having a dog visit your room, set out books with pictures of dogs. Let your children look through the books and compare the pictures of different kinds of dogs.

Touching

Digging Up Bones

Hide several dog bones (available at pet supply stores) in a sand table, a sandbox, or a dishpan of sand. Invite two or three of your children to join you at the sand table. Have them pretend to be dogs. Tell them that they have buried their bones in the sand and now they want to find them. Let them dig in the sand until they have found all their bones.

Sit Up

Talk with your children about how some dogs are trained to follow commands. Show them how dogs sit up, lie down, roll over, beg, shake hands, and speak. Have the children pretend to be dogs. Have them listen to your commands and do the appropriate actions. If you wish, let the children also take turns giving the commands.

Smelling

Follow Your Nose

Tell your children about dogs that are especially good at smelling things. Have them pretend to be dogs and sniff all around the room. What do they smell? Can they smell things that they can't see, like something baking in an oven? What do they think dogs like to smell?

Tasting

Doggy Treats

Cut dog bone shapes out of bread. (Dog bone cookie cutters can sometimes be found at specialty kitchen shops.) Spread the shapes with peanut butter and serve. Let your children pretend they are dogs eating "dog bones."

Birds

Seeing

Bird Feeders

Use this simple idea to make feeders for outside your window. Place several plungers upside down in the ground. Fill one with water and the others with bird seed. Let your children watch the birds at the feeders. How many different birds can they see? Help the children identify as many birds as you can. If you wish, keep a chart that shows how many of each kind of bird the children have seen.

Touching

Bird Nests

Cut up bits of scrap yarn, twine, and string. Let each child have a handful. Mix one part glue with one part water. Pour a small amount of the glue mixture into each child's handful of scraps. Let the children knead the scraps and glue like dough. When they are ready, have each child shape the scrap dough into a ball, then use a thumb to make an indentation in the middle to make a nest. Place the nests on waxed paper to dry. These will harden into beautiful nests. Later, let the children add painted pebbles for eggs.

Bird Songs

While your children are watching the birds in the Bird Feeders activity on the opposite page, have them also listen to the sounds the birds are making. Can they hear the birds calling to each other? How many different bird songs can they hear? If they are very quiet, they might even be able to hear some birds cracking open the sunflower shells to get at the seeds inside. If you wish, have your children listen to a recording of bird calls.

Smelling

Outdoor Scents

Take your children outside. Ask them to pretend to be birds. Have them "fly" around and smell as many different things as they can. Encourage them to smell the grass, flowers, trees, plants, and other things in the yard.

Tasting

Eating Like Birds

Have your children notice how the birds in the Bird Feeders activity on the opposite page are eating. Some birds just sit at the feeder and eat and eat. Have your children pretend to be birds. Have them fly to the snack table. Place a tray of shelled sunflower seeds in the middle of the table. Let your "birds" sit at the table and take a few seeds at a time to eat.

Early Learning Resources

Songs, activities, themes, recipes, and tips

Celebrations

Easy, practical ideas for celebrating holidays and special days around the world. Plus ideas for making ordinary days special.

Celebrating Likes and Differences
Small World Celebrations
Special Day Celebrations
Great Big Holiday Celebrations

Theme-A-Saurus®

Classroom-tested, around-the-curriculum activities organized into imaginative units. Great for implementing child-directed programs.

Multisensory Theme-A-Saurus
Theme-A-Saurus
Theme-A-Saurus II
Toddler Theme-A-Saurus
Alphabet Theme-A-Saurus
Nursery Rhyme Theme-A-Saurus
Storytime Theme-A-Saurus

1•2•3 Series

Open-ended, age-appropriate, cooperative, and no-lose experiences for working with preschool children.

1•2•3 Art
1•2•3 Games
1•2•3 Colors
1•2•3 Puppets
1•2•3 Reading & Writing
1•2•3 Rhymes, Stories & Songs
1•2•3 Math
1•2•3 Science
1•2•3 Shapes

Snacks Series

Easy, educational recipes for healthy eating and expanded learning.

Super Snacks
Healthy Snacks
Teaching Snacks
Multicultural Snacks

Piggyback® Songs

New songs sung to the tunes of childhood favorites. No music to read! Easy for adults and children to learn. Chorded for guitar or autoharp.

Piggyback Songs
More Piggyback Songs
Piggyback Songs for Infants & Toddlers
Piggyback Songs in Praise of God
Piggyback Songs in Praise of Jesus
Holiday Piggyback Songs
Animal Piggyback Songs
Piggyback Songs for School
Piggyback Songs to Sign
Spanish Piggyback Songs
More Piggyback Songs for School

Busy Bees

These seasonal books help two- and three-year-olds discover the world around them through their senses. Each book includes fun activity and learning ideas, songs, snack ideas, and more!

Busy Bees—SPRING
Busy Bees—SUMMER
Busy Bees—FALL
Busy Bees—WINTER

101 Tips for Directors

Great ideas for managing a preschool or daycare. These hassle-free, handy hints are a great help.

Staff and Parent Self-Esteem
Parent Communication
Health and Safety
Marketing Your Center
Resources for You and Your Center
Child Development Training

101 Tips for Toddler Teachers

Designed for adults who work with toddlers.

Classroom Management
Discovery Play
Dramatic Play
Large Motor Play
Small Motor Play
Word Play

101 Tips for Preschool Teachers

Valuable, fresh ideas for adults who work with young children.

Creating Theme Environments
Encouraging Creativity
Developing Motor Skills
Developing Language Skills
Teaching Basic Concepts
Spicing Up Learning Centers

Problem Solving Safari

Designed to help children problem-solve and think for themselves. Each book includes scenarios from children's real play and possible solutions.

Problem Solving Safari—Art
Problem Solving Safari—Blocks
Problem Solving Safari—Dramatic Play
Problem Solving Safari—Manipulatives
Problem Solving Safari—Outdoors
Problem Solving Safari—Science

The Best of Totline® Series

Collections of some of the finest, most useful material published in *Totline Magazine* over the years.

The Best of Totline
The Best of Totline Parent Flyers

Early Learning Resources

Posters, puzzles, and books for parents and children

A Year of Fun

Age-specific books detailing how young children grow and change and what parents can do to lay a foundation for later learning.

Just for Babies
Just for Ones
Just for Twos
Just for Threes
Just for Fours
Just for Fives

Getting Ready for School

Fun, easy-to-follow ideas for developing essential skills that preschoolers need before they can successfully achieve higher levels of learning.

Ready to Learn Colors, Shapes, and Numbers
Ready to Write and Develop Motor Skills
Ready to Read
Ready to Communicate
Ready to Listen and Explore the Senses

Learning Everywhere

Everyday opportunities for teaching children about language, art, science, math, problem solving, self-esteem, and more!

Teaching House
Teaching Town
Teaching Trips

Beginning Fun With Art

Introduce young children to the fun of art while developing coordination skills and building self-confidence.

Craft Sticks • Crayons • Felt
Glue • Paint • Paper Shapes
Modeling Dough • Yarn
Tissue Paper • Scissors
Rubber Stamps • Stickers

Beginning Fun With Science

Make science fun with these quick, safe, easy-to-do activities that lead to discovery and spark the imagination.

Bugs & Butterflies
Plants & Flowers
Magnets
Rainbows & Colors
Sand & Shells
Water & Bubbles

Teaching Tales

Each of these children's books includes a delightful story plus related activity ideas that expand on the story's theme.

Kids Celebrate the Alphabet
Kids Celebrate Numbers

Seeds for Success™

For parents who want to plant the seeds for success in their young children

Growing Creative Kids
Growing Happy Kids
Growing Responsible Kids
Growing Thinking Kids

Learn With Piggyback® Songs

BOOKS AND TAPES
Age-appropriate songs that help children learn!

Songs & Games for Babies
Songs & Games for Toddlers
Songs & Games for Threes
Songs & Games for Fours

Learning Puzzles

Designed to challenge as children grow.

Kids Celebrate Numbers
Kids Celebrate the Alphabet
Bear Hugs 4-in-1 Puzzle Set
Busy Bees 4-in-1 Puzzle Set

Two-Sided Circle Puzzles

Double-sided, giant floor puzzles designed in a circle with cutout pieces for extra learning and fun.

Underwater Adventure
African Adventure

We Work & Play Together Posters

A colorful collection of cuddly bear posters showing adult and children bears playing and working together.

We Build Together
We Cook Together
We Play Together
We Read Together
We Sing Together
We Work Together

Bear Hugs® Health Posters

Encourage young children to develop good health habits. Additional learning activities on back!

We Brush Our Teeth
We Can Exercise
We Cover our Coughs and Sneezes
We Eat Good Food
We Get Our Rest
We Wash Our Hands

Reminder Posters

Photographic examples of children following the rules.

I cover my coughs
I listen quietly
I pick up my toys
I put my things away
I say please and thank you
I share
I use words when I am angry
I wash my hands
I wipe my nose

If you like Totline® Books, you'll love Totline® Magazine!

For fresh ideas that challenge and engage young children in active learning, reach for **Totline Magazine**—Proven ideas from innovative teachers!

Each issue includes

- Seasonal learning themes
- Stories, songs, and rhymes
- Open-ended art projects
- Science explorations
- Reproducible parent pages
- Ready-made teaching materials
- Activities just for toddlers
- Reproducible healthy snack recipes
- Special pull-outs

**Receive a free copy of Totline® Magazine
by calling 800-609-1724 for subscription information.**